Hide Me From ME

"RAB"

Hide Me From ME

"I was designed to inspire, to serve and to love without reservation. I am on a journey to inspire, encourage, empower, and to impact the lives of those who share MY story, but; haven't found THEIR voice!"

TamikaB. and Shaquia Antoinette Barnes

ISBN: 1539330257
ISBN 13: 9781539330257

Dedication

The first woman I would like to dedicate this book to is a woman I had the honor of loving on earth for twenty-four consecutive years! This woman was "My EVERYTHING" and I never imagined that I'd publish a book and not have her next to me to celebrate such an accomplishment. She showed me what peace, love, hope, joy, patience, and fearlessness looked like. She taught me that I couldn't expect everyone to accept me, but; to always be myself. Lastly, she pushed me to walk boldly in who I AM.

Rest Peacefully My Angel
Arnisha Denise Kiah-Akintunde 4/19/1974 – 9/10/2003

The second person that I'm dedicating this book to is a woman who I have loved since our first conversation. I was immediately captivated by her energy, her light and her presence. I have NEVER missed an opportunity to let the world know just how much I love her. This beautiful, charismatic, loving, bold, and authentic woman is not just my OBGYN, she's my light, my accountability partner and a HUGE part of the reason that I am able to tell my story to the world today. Thank you Dr. Maz.

Last but not least, I am dedicating this book to a friend of twenty-two years who inspired me at the age of fifteen to journal my thoughts. She taught me to "Dream big and believe in miracles!"
May her LIGHT shine forever
Rest Eternally "Queen of Light!"

Acknowledgements

Mother,

Thank you for giving birth to me, for nurturing me, for wiping every tear and deflating every fear. Thank you for allowing me to make mistakes in this journey we call life, but; most importantly, thank you for teaching me what the definition of strength is. As a mother who had to serve in dual roles, even with there being the presence of a "father figure" in the home, you are the reason that I will never fail at being a mother to my five beautiful children! You mean the world to me, not just because you gave me life, but; because you labored without an epidural.

Dawn,

Thank you for being a role model and a good friend. Thank you for being my voice of reason and the inspirational force behind me becoming a confident writer. You inspired me.

Tarsha, Ronnessa, Lynette, Channing, Shawan, Russell, Tiffany, Lindsay, Tracy, Twiggy, Shelley, Sha-Sha, The Browns and Mt. Ennon Baptist Church,

Thank you all for supporting me and my children by making sure we had water, electricity, field trip money, a roof over our heads, and spiritual support. When no one else was there, you all were.

Marion Tate, Doris Kiah and Edith Webster,

Thank you for setting a foundation of love that has endured many storms and is still standing.

My aunts (natural and extended) specifically; Delores, Benita and Anita,

Thank you for all that you've done to remind me that I'm not alone and I have a village.

Uncle Tommy,

Thank you for inspiring and motivating me on a daily basis while I worked on this project.

Tierra,

Thank you for being an example of family that's not defined by DNA. Thank you for being loyal, devoted, and a loving little sister. Lastly, thank you for editing this project without altering my message. I love you!

Table of Contents

A Personal Word from TamikaB.

I'm glad that you have decided to take this journey through the life of a mom of multiples, a victim of domestic violence, a former whore-monger, a "whistle-blower," a warrior, but; most importantly a fearless woman of God who understands that the position of "warrior" doesn't come without battle. Hide Me From Me, is a memoir written to motivate, inspire, encourage and inform a multitude of people, regardless of where they are in life. This journey, called "life" has been interesting to say the least. It has been filled with tears, tests, trials, tribulations, testimonies and triumphs. Growing up, I was always taught to "treat others, how you want to be treated," so I have lived my life doing just that. Over the years, I have drawn a wide array of people, from all walks of life from the homeless person whose often times overlooked, to the Presidents/CEO's of fortune 500 companies. Needless to say, I'm so blessed to be surrounded by an overwhelming amount of genuinely good people, who have loved me without reservation.

Whenever I'm asked to describe myself, the first three words that come to mind are fun, loving and energetic. Because of the way I was raised, no one person held any more value than the other. My mother believed that you should see the heart of a person and not the possessions they hold. I was raised by a strong woman who I contribute my strength and courage to. She is one of the most amazing women I know. She too was raised by an amazing woman (my natural grandmother) who derived from a strong breed of women, and a foundation authenticated by love. Even having been raised by such a wonderful woman, and having been taught all the right things, didn't stop me from making choices that would lead to a failed marriage, a broken heart, multiple failed relationships, Sexually Transmitted Diseases, near death experiences and betrayal.

Have you ever encountered someone who says those things, that often times become unspoken words? In this memoir, you'll discover that I'm transparent and determined to leave it all in this book. You'll get the good, the bad, the ugly, the embarrassing, the brass truth, and the uncomfortable. You will also read some of the most difficult moments I've ever had to face.

Bright Spot

> "Your beauty should not come from outward adornment, such as braided hair and the wearing of gold jewelry and fine clothes. Instead, it should be that of your inner self, the unfading beauty of a gentle and quiet spirit, which is of great worth in God's sight."
> 1 PETER 3:3-4

I believe that a virtuous woman's identity on the inside must be reflected by a righteous walk. When she enters into a room, there should be "something" that immediately sets her apart from others. There will be a light and an anointing that flows from the inside out. It will be unknown because that "something" is the presence of God. As you may already know, GOD can never be explained and His power can't be captured into words or a phrase. As a virtuous woman, often times I serve as that bright-spot in darkness. Darkness is generally referred to as a place that has no light that prevents one's ability to see where you are, who's around you or where you're going. As you know, light is the total opposite of darkness and represents guidance and one's ability to see clearly. Metaphorically, all we need to see in darkness is light! This light can come in the form of a warm smile, eye contact; words of encouragement, motivation or an expressed genuine interest. People are always looking for that something or someone who makes them feel alive! They're looking for that person who's capable of bringing life to what appears to be a dead situation.

I was born Tamika Yvette Benbow, but; over the years, I've acquired nicknames which in my opinion are names of affection and adoration. When I was a little girl, my extended Aunts gave me the nickname "Batmite" (a popular cartoon character in the1980s). To this very day, I'm not sure why they called me that. When I was in my early teenage years, my oldest brother gave me the nickname "Big Mix," which I have tattooed on my upper left arm. My brother and cousins called my cousin Nikki "Mix" so I was "Big Mix" because although she was older, I was bigger than she was. Nikki and I were inseparable until we entered our late teenage years. I looked up to her and every chance I got I wanted to be around her, so to have a nickname that mirrored hers was alright with me. As I entered into adulthood, I grew out of those adolescent nicknames, but; it didn't stop my brother from calling me "Big Mix" nor did it stop my Aunts, Uncle and Cousins from calling me "Batmite."

As an adult in 2008 I met a woman (who I'll call "Becky") that played a significant role in my life for a short period of time. This would prove to be one of the most enjoyable and life altering seasons on my life. It was then that I acquired the nickname "Sunshine" [as she called me] which was more suitable than "Batmite" or "Big Mix." In my opinion, Sunshine is the representation of life which is produced by power given from the rays of sunlight. I believe that it also represents a bright-spot in a place or situation where weariness, darkness and sadness inhabit. As long as I could remember, people have told me that I have a tendency to brighten the days of others. I would literally walk into a room and my positive energy would radiate throughout the room and permeate in the lives of those around me. Sunshine became my name in the office amongst those who were a part of our inner circle. I would come into the office and have sticky notes on my monitor that would say things like "Hey Sunshine, I miss you" or "Sunshine call me when you get in" and I knew it had to either be Becky, My TiTi or one of those closest to us.

In 2009, when I found out I was pregnant with my 5th child, I was forced to find a new OBGYN because my doctor decided to close his practice without warning so he referred me to a new OBYN, in Fort Washington, MD. When I first met her, I immediately fell in love with her spirit because she was kind, warm, very informative, and had the most amazing bedside manner I'd ever received. During my 3rd or 4th visit, she walked in the examination room and said, "how are you feeling today Sunshine?" Immediately, I was elated that these two women, who had never encountered one another, saw something in me that could only be summed up in a compound word. I recall her saying to me one day, "You have a magnetic energy that touches the lives of anyone who comes in contact with you." Those words served as a reminder that we are remembered by the way we love and the energy that we share. What we wear, who we know and where we shop, work and dine, doesn't define who we are as individuals. If we carry a positive energy, then we become positive people. If we become positive people, we will attract positive people, transfer that energy and transform negativity.

Energy doesn't lie and my energy has transferred into the lives of others. Often times, people couldn't tell when I was sad, in pain, frustrated nor depressed because I kept a smile on my face. I refused to look like what I was going through during those periods of darkness. Truth be told, I couldn't allow my feelings to emerge because there were people who looked to me for encouragement, comfort, motivation, support or to always be that "bright spot" that got them through the next minute, hour, day or week even. Then there were those who were sitting back watching [spectators] me in anticipation of witnessing me fail. This gave me more of a reason to go harder because I was determined to finish stronger.

Let's Get NAKED

**"Remember in order to walk into the fullness of
your gift you must first walk in YOUR TRUTH."**

The phrase "let's get naked" can be taken a couple of different ways depending on the individual and their mindset. Nearly six years ago, if someone were to say to me "let's get naked" my first thought would've been to get completely nude. Not just because of the definition of the word naked, but; because of my state of mind during that particular time. Today, when I think of the word "naked" the first thing that comes to mind is being exposed. The second thing that comes to mind is being transparent even when it's uncomfortable. Lastly, when I think of being "naked" I think of being vulnerable. Personally, I love being vulnerable because it allows others to get a real, raw and unfiltered view of who I am. Over the course of the last decade, I've learned that it's safer for me to be myself than it is to send a representative. I've always been a secure woman who found it easy to express myself. One of my old co-workers would consistently remind me that it was ok to be real, but; I needed to find a filter. So, although I loved expressing myself, I understood that I was obligated to protect the message that I was attempting to deliver. In an effort to cater to other people's feelings and to make sure I was delivering an authentic message, I decided to work on my delivery. What I've learned over the years is that filtering is simply another way of saying "I respect you." There were times that

I found this difficult to do because I didn't know how to be anything besides real.

I believe that people prefer authentic even when they can't afford it. I'd rather have authentic over a knock off any day. Metaphorically speaking, I believe that your walk is bold when you know that you're wearing the real deal. As I began sharing my story I had to consider that I walk in my reality verses living in theory, which is what most people do. I had to prepare for the uncomfortable moments that will come after I elect to unveil my truth. More times than not people are comfortable with being ignorant because it allows them to remain in a state of familiarity. It allows them to remain uneducated, misinformed and secure. In my opinion, we become comfortable with what is offered to us as truth and never desire more because we aren't ready to accept the reality of our situations. What I realized about myself was that when I began to walk in my truth, it invoked progression in various areas of my life, especially spiritually and mentally. The direction of my life was much clearer and my purpose became evident. I spent more time walking in my purpose and less time focusing on my past. I began a journey to evolution that would prove to be more challenging than I envisioned. Parenting, work, my health and simply finding balance became more of a challenge because I looked at life through a brand new pair of eyes. For instance, as a single mom I had to deal with my reality when I was forced to sit my children down and explain to them the severity of my medical element and that it can result in sudden death. I elected to prepare my children for the worst case scenario (from the youngest to the oldest) because the last thing I wanted was for something to happen to me and my babies weren't prepared. Although you can never prepare for death, I felt like I could help them understand "WHY." I taught them how to administer me medication and we designed an emergency plan just in case something happened. Preparing my children for a possible tragedy was uncomfortable, BUT;

it was necessary. I find that the easiest way to deal with something or someone is to know exactly what or who you're dealing with.

I used to feel like I was being too liberal and that people had a difficult time accepting me because of it, but; then I realized that some people are too guarded and bothered by those things that they have absolutely no control over. I'm the woman that generally says (out loud) what others are thinking, but; are too afraid to say. Although I love being completely naked from a literal perspective, I found FULL enjoyment of being unclothed when I realized that being "naked" is simply being transparent. Transparency allows others to make an educated choice as to whether they are willing to accept both you and your circumstances. I believe that being vulnerable and transparent is your way of saying, "I trust you." For example, I recall a time when I would prefer the lights off and I would keep my t-shirt on during sex. I would do this because I wasn't comfortable and didn't trust my partner(s) enough to get completely naked initially. The natural eye only gives you a limited view and the unfortunate reality is that people judge based on what they initially see.

Unless you allow these individuals in, the real scars and wounds will remain invisible. I believe people hold back because they're afraid of rejection, failure and the "fear of the unknown." When you walk in fear, you hold back that which will naturally escape you and you risk missing opportunities of a lifetime. The biggest being an opportunity to LIVE!

They Ruined Me, So I Ruined Them

The night I lost my virginity was when I first discovered how weak the flesh is and the importance of self-control. I also learned that no matter how many times my mother stressed the importance of staying pure; I was going to do what felt good to me in that moment verses what was good for me. When I lost my virginity, it was to a man that was thirteen years my senior. At the tender age of fourteen, I met a twenty-seven-year-old man. It was not long after I graduated from the ninth grade, in Washington, DC. We were headed into summer break, so I went to spend the weekend over my brother's house in Temple Hills, MD. I remember it like it was yesterday. It was a hot Saturday afternoon in the early summer of 1994, I decided to walk over to the grocery store, in Marlow Heights to get something to snack on while I was waiting for my sister (who was living with my brother at the time) to get off of work. I almost never walked alone because my mother always stressed that there is safety in numbers, but; on this particular day I was by myself. On the way back to my brother's house, a gold BMW Station Wagon with dark tinted windows pulled up next to me and came to a complete stop. Since I was a fearless and curious young lady, I stopped and gave a feisty look. I mean I was born and raised in Southeast, D.C. and saw it all, so I wasn't afraid.

The passenger window of the car starts to roll down and immediately I felt even more comfortable because I observed that there was only one person in car. It was a light-skinned handsome brother with

TamikaB. and Shaquia Antoinette Barnes

a well maintained beard. Now, I wasn't attracted to anything besides dark-skinned brothers at that time, but; there was no harm in speaking. The dude shouted out of the window.

The Dude: A
Me: B
The Dude: You real funny beautiful, what's your name?
Me: Mika.
The Dude: Where you going in that white dress Mika?
Me: Why?
The Dude: Maybe I wanna give you a ride.
Me: I don't need one, I'm not going far.
The Dude: Can I call you?
Me: You look old, I'm only 14 years old and my sister said old men give girls worms.
The Dude: I don't believe that and I'm only 27.
Me: So and 27 is super old.
The Dude: Well, my name is "Blake" can I give you my number?
Me: Sure, but; I'm not giving you mine.

At this point, I guess he figured out that I still wasn't going to approach his car so he gets out of the car. I was glad that he did because me being both young and immature, I was definitely interested in seeing his shoes. My sister always told me to look at a dude's shoes first and then his fingernails, which tells you a lot about his upkeep. Although I was fully developed, I was still your typical fourteen-year-old girl because all of the superficial things about him jumped out at me when he stepped out of his car. His shoes were fresh, he was fly, his fingernails were well manicured, he smelled awesome, and his haircut was on point. I wasn't concerned with the fact that this twenty-seven-year-old man was trying to talk to a fourteen-year-old girl although it was both illegal and immoral. As a mom of two young girls, I'd even add disgusting to that list of concerns that were irrelevant to me at that time.

He handed me his phone number which was written on a piece of brown paper bag, and said "please promise you're going to call me." I grabbed the number and said I will, but; not until I get home tomorrow. My brother didn't play, so I wasn't going to take that risk calling him from my brother's house. The next day came and I called him from my house phone when my mom and stepfather left the house. While my mom allowed me to talk to boys, she still tried to closely monitor who I communicated with. She also instilled an honest fear in me so I knew my limits, but; I was still curious and pushed the envelope at times just to see how much I could get away with. After only two weeks of talking to Blake, he asked me to come visit me. It was a Friday night and my mom and dad (who I call Pop) were at the racetrack, which was their Friday ritual sometimes. I knew that they would get back pretty late so I gave him directions and he was there within 30 minutes. Before he came, I told him that I was only coming out to sit in the car to talk and nothing more. I was a little scared of getting caught so I put my younger sister Stella on lookout. I told her that if they came back to tell them that I went to the mailbox.

Blake pulls up and I went outside and got into his car. We sat there talking about various things and as sure as I feared, after about twenty minutes of sitting in his car, I heard the pipes on Pop's car pulling up and I told Blake to pull off. He did so without hesitation and he pulled into a parking lot of a nearby apartment complex. He parked in a secluded area where there were only about three cars. I told him that I was about to walk back because my mother isn't stupid and she was going to come looking for me. It wasn't like we went far from my house. We were only one street over. He assured me that he would take me back and that they wouldn't be suspicious. I was so gullible and trusted him. While we were sitting there talking, he leaned over and started kissing me, and then slid his hands down my shorts. His hand slid straight back to my anal area and all I heard him say was "got damn." He instantly pulled his hand out of my shorts and started to unbuckle his belt and pants. It was like he was so excited that he became extremely aggressive. He reached over and pulled one of my breasts out and began to gently lick my nipples and suck on my breast. He started grabbing my inner thighs. After about two minutes of sucking my breast, he looked at me and said "can I please put it in just one time?" I looked at him and said I'm a virgin, and I don't want to mess up your car. I was told that when you lose your virginity, it can be pretty messy. He paused, looked at me and then said, "Can I at least feel it again?" By this time, I was extremely aroused, my vagina was throbbing and I wanted to let him play with it so I replied, "yes." He reached on the side of my seat and adjusted my seat, and then he pulled my shorts and my panties down and became aggressive again. He was rubbing my vagina hard and fast, which didn't feel as good as it did the first time he rubbed it so I said, "that's enough." He looked at me and started sucking his fingers that were just inside of me and kept saying, "please let me feel it." While he was begging he climbed on my side, moved my left leg, and pulled his penis out. I didn't want to look down at it because I didn't want to get scared if his penis was too large. I closed my eyes, and tried to brace myself for what was about to happen. He gently slid it in and after about 5 strokes, he buried his face in my breast, started growling and his body was jerking. He had ejaculated inside of me, climbed back on his side and buttoned his pants back up. I was confused because it didn't hurt at all and it was over as soon as it started. I pulled my shorts and panties up, fixed my shirt, and told him to hurry up and drop me at the corner. I had just given him my gift and the most intimate part of me as a woman. At that moment I experienced a flood of emotions because I had just allowed this grown man to take the most innocent part of who I was and it didn't last more than a minute. In that moment, I was so scared to face my mother, upset that I had just given up my gift, and annoyed that it was over so quickly. I wanted to cry, but; I had to get it together because I didn't want my mother to know that I had just lost my virginity. He dropped me at the corner and I walked as fast as I could to get to my house. This felt like the longest walk ever. The moment I walked through the door my mother asked me where I had been and I made the mistake of saying "I went to the mailbox." My father (who was a postal worker for more than thirteen years at the time) chimed in and said "I'm the mother fucking mailman," but; my mother didn't say a word, she just slapped me in the face and the beating followed. I was surprised that I wasn't bleeding and hurting after he took my virginity, but; I was glad because I was scared to go take a shower immediately. I didn't want my mother to get suspicious and think that I had sex.

After my mom calmed down a little, I finally told her the truth, well a part of it anyway. I confessed that I was in a guy's car and that I was just talking to him and told him to pull off when I heard them pull up. She asked me a lot of questions and I did a lot of lying. The first question she asked was "how old is he?" This was the one thing that I never lied to her about. I told her that Blake was twenty-seven years old and that he knew that I was fourteen. In the middle of us talking, the house phone rang and it was him. My mother gave me a firm look and grabbed the phone. My heart was beating fast as I sat on my bed listening to my mom talk to him in the hallway. He held a conversation with my mom for more than ten minutes, and I was angry just listening. Although he never mentioned to my mom that we had sex, he did tell her that I told him that I was seventeen years old. I was so hurt that my mother believed him over me, but; I had just given her the worst story ever and disrespected her, so she had every reason not to believe me. While they continued to talk, I just laid on my bed, cried and replayed in my mind what had just occurred in that dark parking lot. I was sad for a couple of days, but; that sadness quickly turned to rage. That rage was the beginning of my revenge, which would go on for more than a decade and a half (off and on). I was angry because I was smitten over a guy that I went to school with and I would've rather had given myself to "Bruiser" than to Blake. Most importantly I was mad that I disrespected my mom for this coward.

Needless to say, I was forbidden from talking to Blake ever again and I was ok with that. He on the other hand wasn't okay. Not only did he call my house all the time, but; even after we relocated from Southeast, DC to Greenbelt, MD, he found me again. By this time, I was fifteen and I had regained my mom's trust so I actually had my own phone line. When we relocated my mother elected to have our old number announce the new number. One afternoon, Blake called and Stella answered the phone. She gave Blake my phone number and that's when the trouble began. Up until this point I had successfully ignored him. He would call all night long at this time in my life; I had a boyfriend that I loved, so I would ignore his calls all the time. The one time I decided to hold a conversation with him, he asked me a million questions. One of his first questions was what school did I go to now and I made the mistake of telling him. The very next day, I was getting on the school bus to go home when I felt someone grab my hand and it was Blake. He asked me to come with him because he just wanted to talk. He promised to take me home as soon as we were done talking. This time he kept his word. We didn't have sex and this would be the very last time that we spoke. I said some of the most disrespectful, hurtful and demoralizing things to him on this car ride from school to my house (which was ten minutes away). He apologized for lying to my mom, he apologized for taking my virginity, and then when he began to cry, I told him that I needed to go in the house because my boyfriend was waiting for me to call him to let him know I was home. This wasn't true, but; I wanted him to know what it felt like to be hurt and empty.

After that emotionally draining car ride, I avoided every phone call and every attempt he made to communicate. He would show up at my school and be waiting in the parking lot at least twice a week until I told him that I was going to tell my mother everything. After all, he stood to lose a lot, especially his freedom, if my mother found out that he took my virginity. He was a father of two and a DC police officer. After that threat, he stopped showing up at my school and the calls slowed down and eventually stopped.

What I realized the moment I lost my purity is that I lost my respect for men in general. It was already difficult for me to trust men, especially since my biological father consistently disappointed me and failed me as a father. That feeling of being neglected by the man who helped to create me was indescribable. I felt like I needed him there to guide me and to protect me from the Blake's of the world. That night I lost so much more than my virginity. I lost my innocence, my soul, my value, and my ability to love. I also lost respect for myself.

Well, you know what they say about people who have been hurt? They generally turn around and hurt other people. So I began to hurt men, starting with Blake. It was during this time that I realized that sex, lies, betrayal and manipulation would become my weapon and every man that I would come in contact with was going to forever remember any encounter that he had with me. They were going to pay for what I allowed him to do to me in that dark parking lot on that hot summer night.

When I was molested, I was only eleven and it was by an extended relative. When it happened, I pretended I was asleep and when he left out of the room, I woke my older cousin up and asked her to call my mother. When my mother came to get me, she went off and I never went back over my aunt's house without my mother. Always remember that suppressed abuse can be detrimental to growth, trust, and future relationships. Between the man who molested me, my absent father and the grown man who took my virginity, they ruined me, so I ruined them.

For Me, Life is Like Football

Always remember "If you play FOOTBALL to become a millionaire, then you'll be just that, but; if you play because you love the game & believe in the magic of football, then you'll become LEGENDARY!"

When it comes to sports, football has and will always be my first love! I've always felt like I could relate much of my life to the sport itself. Football is not just a sport; it's a lifestyle that teaches a wide array of things to include life skills, strength, faith, agility, and much more. My daughter (Heaven) loves football just like her mom and elected to play tackle at just six years old. At almost ten years old, she's entering into her fourth season this year and I'm excited about it. I'm excited that she fearlessly elected to play a male dominated sport. My son Rashard (Torpedo) plays with his heart and leaves it all on the field. He's played several positions, but; loves playing "Corner" because it's the position where he's most comfortable. In the four seasons that they've been playing, the game has made them laugh, cry, scream but most importantly it's encouraged them both to commit like never before. It's tested their strength, skills, endurance, loyalty and patience. We have built some amazing relationships in the football realm and have gained extended family. I also gained a greater respect for "Team Moms" as I learned that being a team mom required me to go from being a mom of five to a mom of more than thirty-seven in one season. As a "Team Mom" you become a mom, logistics coordinator, budget analyst, cleaners, seamstress, nurse, mediator and referee at times. But, the reward was much greater than the responsibility itself. This up-coming season is going to be epic as I have four children playing this year. As they continue to learn the fundamentals of football I hope that they NEVER lose their unfiltered love for the game and take away all of the lessons the game offers!

"What I find interesting is that my son has taken so many lessons away from the game already and shares them with me every chance he gets. One night while watching a game, he turned to me and said **"people can know your plays, but; what makes them successful is their ability to stop your play."** That was so deep to me and I imme-diately thought to myself, it's a lot like success.

Like life, I believe that **"there's a big moment that can change the direction of the game."** Life for me was great and my life was on course until the day I "Blew the Whistle" on the government. That one decision to do what was right changed the direction of my career, life and health. I went from having it all together to being homeless, broke and sicker than I had ever been before in my life. I always tell people "sometimes to do what is right, requires us to do what is uncomfortable."

In both life and football, **"you can never make a group decision with an individual mindset."** When my cousin had a massive stroke and brain aneurism, we spent nearly two consecutive weeks in the ICU Family Room around the clock. While in there, I met a man who was with a large family whose loved one was on life support. I recall having a conversation with him about the family making a decision to pull the plug. To him, it seemed as if some of his family members were thinking of themselves versus thinking about what was best for their loved one who had been fighting for his life for months. When you're responsible for making a group decision, you have to set aside personal feelings and emotions. You have to be capable of separating the facts from your own feelings. This also applies in the game of football as well. Think about it for a minute. When a team huddles before a play, every man has a position and a task. There is generally a play that's called in the huddle and when that huddle breaks, there is an expectation that every player is ready to execute that play. If one man leaves that huddle with an individual mindset and doesn't follow the play, then the play won't be as effective as it would've been when they left the huddle.

"Those who go harder, finish stronger" seems like a cliché saying, but; it's the truth! I have applied this to my workout regimen, football, parenting, praying, etc. I also teach my children this because when they realize that hard work pays off, then they've learned that nothing worth having comes easy.

I remember my sons first season of tackle football like it was yesterday. He was playing 8U (8 unlimited) which was a developmental team of thirty-two boys. Our young athletes lost every scrimmage during the preseason and parents were probably more frustrated than the children and coaches. I was talking to one of the parents and I recall telling her that **"taking a loss, teaches you how to win."** She looked at me and said, you may be right, but; I'm still mad as hell. I just laughed and said okay. I never doubted our boys' abilities, especially since I watched these boys practice rain or shine, in flaming temperatures, and while sick (literally). Just before our first game while standing on the sideline, I looked at my boys and said, "Do you guys like the way losing felt?" They relied, "NO" and I said, "Well now that y'all know what losing feels like, you're ready to win." Our 8U developmental team went through their season **UNDEFEATED,** and they won both the Division and the Championship! They played in inclement weather and blew a couple of teams out scoring more than fifty-four points to zero. Our boys took all of their pre-season losses and learned how to win in the process. They also learned that **"You should never care who your opponent is, ALWAYS, play to win!"** We had a few boys of size, but; we went up against a few of larger, skilled teams and our boys were never intimidated by their opponent's sizes. They would hit the field, ready to play as a team and WON every game!

While winning was fun and the boys were having the time of their lives, the most memorable part for me was watching men inspire, encourage and motivate our children day-after-day. I enjoyed watching them grow stronger together and I also enjoyed watching them develop bonds that still remain to this day. During our season with the Silver Hill Bears, we built relationships that have proven to be long lasting. I acquired several new sisters, a few new brothers and my children adopted numerous aunts and uncles along the way like Coach Donnie, who quickly became role models for my boys and Heaven's favorite coach.

Heaven & Coach Donnie (Former Football Commissioner)

"WHEN YOU'RE WINNING, EVERYONE IS WATCHING!"

Baby Momma's and Drama

In my opinion, a "Baby Momma" is a label given to a woman who has a child or children by a man with whom she isn't married to or estranged from. I've always loathed this label as it comes with such a negative connotation and is often times used by the ex, the ex's new woman or the family of the ex. I'm a woman who's referred to as the "baby momma" and the ex-wife. Contrary to what society portrays, being a baby momma isn't cute. I am the mother of five children and yes I believe there is a distinct difference between being a Baby Momma and being the mother of his child. I have encountered a few "Baby Mommas" in my lifetime and then I have met exes and the mother of a man's child. I'm certainly not a baby momma and I don't allow my exes to reduce me to what society portrays as being acceptable.

When I first met my youngest son's brother and his mother, I was probably more excited than my son was to meet them. My ex would constantly say "my Baby Momma is crazy so I don't think it's a good idea for y'all to meet." He would beg me to leave it alone, but; I believe that when you have children, you have to establish some type of relationship for the sake of the children especially when the fathers aren't consistently in the picture. After meeting Ice (the mother of my son's older brother), I discovered that he was wrong and to this day we keep in contact. We have never had an argument, disagreement nor did we allow our children's dad to create a wedge between us. We genuinely care for one another and the welfare of all of our children. I contribute the dynamics of our relationship to the fact that it's all about the children for us. We are responsible adults and neither of us wanted to be with the dad.

There are so many different types of "Baby Mommas" and while many embrace it as if it's some type of accomplishment, I simply don't care for it. Just because you aren't in a relationship with the woman doesn't give you the right to demean her in any way. Just before my ex (Wink) and I began dating; he was casually dating someone else. Just three months into our relationship, the woman he was dating called him to tell him that she was pregnant. It was difficult for him to tell me in the beginning, and when he finally did, he literally begged me not to leave him. He kept saying she's just my "Baby Mother," and nothing more. While I actually believed him, I knew that I could never compete with a baby and because he didn't have children, I wanted this to be the most joyful experience for him. Based on the two encounters that I had with this woman, I knew that she was going to be a problem throughout her pregnancy and after the baby arrived. I explained to him that I hated the term "Baby Momma" and that he really needed to try and work things out with her for the sake of this unborn child. Needless to say he and I mutually decided to separate and to remain friends. He is Heaven's (my daughter) godfather, so I knew that we had to maintain a good healthy relationship for the sake of her.

The most uncomfortable experience that I ever had was with the mother of my two step-daughters. When I began dating their father, I didn't have any children and didn't have a desire to have any. We did everything together and I always encouraged him to spend time with his children because I have a huge family and wanted to make them a part of it. His daughters' mother was very vindictive and would do things like pop up at our home, call to spark up an argument, and pretend the children were sick in the middle of the night and claim to need medicine, so that he had to come out. She would express that because

I didn't have any children, she felt like I was incapable of taking care of her three and eight-year-old daughters. I knew her problem was the fact that I was eighteen years old, educated, goal oriented and working two jobs (which was something that she wasn't doing). I was in a serious relationship with the man she wanted to be with. She was intimidated, jealous, hurt, selfish, a welfare recipient and angry that he had moved on after she had given him children. Not only did he leave her after she gave him children and more than a decade of her life, but; then he turned around and married me after only courting me for one year. This added salt to the wound that he created. Her anger towards him had become so problematic that she started to use her children as leverage. She would make him come in and get the children and then try to have sex with him so that she had something to use against him. I don't mind dealing with the mothers of children, but; I don't like women who use their children as pawns. So, as his wife, I immediately interceded. Two years after meeting me, she would quickly learn that I was a sharp twenty-year-old, who loved children regardless of whether I gave birth to them or not. I filed the necessary paperwork with the courts for visitation because I understood what my husband didn't and that was that child support and visitation were two separate issues. We deserved to love them without having to deal with her constant shenanigans. During a visitation pickup on a Friday evening, my husband realized that my nine-year-old step-daughter had a black eye. Her mother punched her in the eye and then wrote a note to the school fabricating a story about her playing football with cousins. After we discovered that she was abusing her, I contacted authorities and went through the judicial process for sole physical and legal custody. I involved Child Protective Services, and allowed my mother to sit with her through the interview because she felt more comfortable talking to the investigator in my mother's presence. I felt a flood of emotions and wanted to give her a piece of my mind, especially since the reason she gave her the black eye was because she couldn't read a word. We discovered my stepdaughter had a learning disability through testing and we found out that her mother had been doing her work for her at home. We got tired of fighting her in court. Getting weary was ok, but; we refused to give up. I knew eventually she would show the courts who she really was as a person. Well after the physical abuse against my stepdaughter and a psychological evaluation of me, my husband (at the time) and their Mom, the courts found me to be "the most-fit individual to raise the children." I wasn't surprised because although I was only twenty, I had a lot going for myself and I came from a good family. Eventually after the marriage dissolved, I divorced my husband, but; my mom always said we don't divorce children. I kept both of my stepdaughters until I got tired of fighting with their mother and not getting any support from my ex-husband. I had moved on with my life and was six months pregnant with my second child when I was being dragged to court every other month. I was still awarded joint custody, but; because my step children's mother was bitter, she kept blocking my phone numbers and wouldn't let me see the children. As a mother I understood a little more as to why she tried to use every avenue possible, but; what I never understood was why she hurt her children in the process. Everything that we (as women) do to hurt the man who helped us to create will adversely impact our children and sometimes those around us as well.

A small part of me was happy that I stopped trying because I found peace when I did. I focused on my family and kept them lifted in prayer. We are unaware of God's plan for our lives and none of us expected what happened. She passed away several years after she got them back, so I was glad that they had that time with her to mend their relationships before God called her home. When a man has a child by a woman, she then becomes the mother of this child, not a "Baby Momma." She is due a certain level of respect whether it is in the presence of the child or not. Her position as the mother of his child should never be demeaned in anyway even if her behavior is contrary to what it should be.

Check Your Man, Not Her

*M*en and women view cheating from two different perspectives. In my opinion, infidelity is not just a physical act, but; mental, emotional and spiritual as well. As a husband or wife, if you've ever become vulnerable to the opposite sex in any way, you've violated your covenant. If you have desired someone other than your spouse, then you have committed the act itself (in the eyes of God.) For a husband, understanding who God wants him to be is paramount in becoming who he needs to be for the wife that he deserves. The position of a husband is to love, cover, protect, and provide, but; before he can do any of these he must have a solid relationship with God. He must also understand that he has an unwavering responsibility to his family and he must possess resources to take care of that family. Lastly, he must acknowledge that as a husband (coverer), he's restricted from worldly behaviors and violating the institution of marriage.

In my opinion, the position of a wife is to love, honor, serve, and submit. As an ex-wife of a man who didn't have a relationship with God, I learned the real definition of being "unequally yoked." In coaching married couples, I realized that you can be married to another Christian and still be "unequally yoked." This causes issues in the marriage and eventually creates opportunities for one or both people to step outside of the marriage for comfort. In any relation-ship, regardless of whether it's a friendship, courtship, partnership or marriage, communication is pivotal. You must be able to effectively communicate about any and everything. As a wife I learned that the secret in talking to your husband is listening and the key to listening is paying attention to those things that are left unsaid. I can recall receiving a text message from a woman early one morning because I had been communicating with her husband ("Dope Boy.") This woman, who had left her husband and relocated to another household months prior to contacting me, was checking his phone bill and became concerned that he was cheating on her AGAIN (as she stated) because of our lengthy conversations. Her estranged husband, whom I dated eighteen-years prior, lied and told her that I was his therapist. His wife began to explain to me that he had cheated on her with a woman who would just "give him head" and then went on to say "I know why he cheated with her, because I haven't given him head in thirteen years." Well, let's make something clear. What you will NOT do, what you do NOT or can NOT do, someone else will. Needless to say, me, being the unfiltered woman that I am, I explained to this woman that it was nearly impossible to save her marriage from a different residence. I also explained to her that even if she managed to save her marriage, it was going to be weak and constant turmoil because of the deeply rooted issues that existed. She was angry with me and like most angry wives, she lashed out. Why? The reality is, withholding sex from your husband isn't going to make him do right, but; it may provoke him to do something or someone else. It may make him turn to pornography, which can be worse than turning to another woman. It's been my experience that once a man becomes attached to watching pornography and uses it as an outlet; you will begin to lose his attention sexually. He will have an increased desire to fulfill what's trapped in his mind. Often times, he's not captured by the woman he watches, but; by what she's actually doing while he's watching her. It may also make him run to another woman who will give him what his partner refuses to. In this case, Dope boy's wife refused to perform oral sex, so he found someone who would.

<u>Let's Examine This For A Minute:</u>

"The other woman" is always viewed in a negative light...rightfully so. As a married woman, you can be upset with "the other woman." BUT WHY? Because she's morally wrong for sleeping with a married man (if she even knew he was married)? Because she could potentially break up your "happy or not so happy home?" Or perhaps, you should be upset with her because YOUR husband (who you entered into a covenant with) chose her? My point is "the other woman" isn't your problem because she isn't a part of your covenant. The problem is with your "Covering" AKA [your husband.]

"She understands that a man's flesh doesn't know the difference between his wife and his concubine."

I quickly discovered that when a man falls in love with the true essence of a woman, he will have a desire to secure her. Some men fall in love with the idea of loving a woman and will move forward full steam ahead until he realizes that it wasn't a good idea. Then there are men who simply fall in love with the things that a woman does for him in one or more areas of his life. In these instances, I believe she becomes the other woman. Honestly speaking, I've been in all three of the aforementioned situations and back in the day I enjoyed the position of being the other woman more than any of the others. I was the woman who was secured by a man after a brief courtship and I was an amazing wife to a man who was undeserving of me which turned me completely off. There were nights when he would beat me and I vowed to never remarry again after I gathered the courage to leave him. I've had men who were in love with the idea of loving me until they realized that I wasn't their ideal woman. In my opinion, these men didn't understand what it was that they actually deserved. They just knew what they desired and in that moment it was me.

During a time in my life when I was trying to serve two masters, I did the things that other women pretended they didn't do. I was the woman who was discreet, unfiltered, fun, understanding, loyal and uninhibited, so I became 'the other woman" various times over a five-year period. I was the emotional, physical and in one case spiritual connection that they needed, but; wasn't getting from their wives. I had the ability to hear unspoken words. I catered to sexual desires that they didn't quite understand existed. I handled business for them in a moment's notice and I even prayed for them consistently because during that season I believed that serving two masters was possible, just not at the same time. Having my way with these men and killing their spirits became easy. I got what I wanted, gave them what they needed and walked away when it was time. There were multiple married men and many sleepless nights. I nearly ruined families and after contracting a curable sexually transmitted disease from one of them, I almost went to prison.

Although I viewed marriage differently after the abuse I experienced for more than six consecutive years, I still viewed marriage as sacred grounds. I used to pride myself on not entertaining nor engaging in any inappropriate behavior with a man who was married, legally separated or even involved (in a relationship). I would turn down a married man in a heartbeat and then counsel him immediately following. All of that changed after I attended a Super Bowl party at my girlfriend Becky's house. That was the day I met DP! When I arrived at her house, I walked around speaking to people and introducing myself to those people that I didn't know. When I walked in the kitchen, there was a small group of brothers who didn't look familiar so I approached them. As I extended my hand to one brother, he said "Tamika Gass right?!" I said, "How'd you know" and he replied, "I've seen you on Becky's timeline." Needless to say, before I left there, DP and I discovered that there was an undeniable chemistry. I saw that he was wearing a wedding band, but; I wasn't going to start asking questions because despite the chemistry, I didn't plan to communicate with him beyond that night. We left the party at the same time, and after an innocent hug, we parted ways. Just an hour after leaving Becky's house, I received an instant message from him on Facebook. He was making sure that I made it home safely. After communicating through social media for a couple of months, DP and I developed a friendship that would later evolve after I joined a group chat that he was a part of. This group chat was cool and nothing was off the table for discussion. DP and I flirted in the group, through instant message on social media and through text messaging.

One afternoon, while going back and forth in the group chat, I received a text message from DP letting me know that he was going to be free (his wife was going to be out of town for a week) and that he wanted to see me. I planned to take total advantage of the opportunity to see him, so, later that evening I sent him my address and he was there within a couple of hours. The door was unlocked so he let himself in. He walked up the stairs and came over to where I was sitting. I stood up to greet him with a hug, but; he kissed me and at that moment I knew that our night would be great. Personally, I can tell a lot about a man by the way he kisses. I was watching Monday Night Football when DP got there, and nothing ever distracts me from football, but; DP managed to. The way he smelled was a distraction in itself. He looked at me and said, "So are you going to show me your bedroom?" I laughed because that was the first time I actually heard someone use that line. Right after I laughed, I stood back up and walked him straight back to my bedroom. I was already excited after that kiss and he was about to find out just how excited I was. Kissing, in my opinion is very intimate so I didn't kiss all of my partners. The kissing started and we both began to undress one another. I asked him to lie down and I recall saying to him, "Are you ready?" He looked at me and said yes! That was my queue to give DP exactly what he needed from me in that moment. I began to kiss him, gently moving from his lips to his lower extremity. I knew that he needed me to handle him with care, so I took my time. He experienced my fascination with saliva as began to spit on him, consuming all of him. My neck began to take on a range and motion that I didn't recall being capable of. After engaging in that memorable four-play, we began to make love. This involved unprotected penetration, licking, sucking, caressing, kissing and unforgettable motion. The very first time was so intense that he never attempted to pull out when he climaxed. That was very risky considering I'm an extremely fertile woman, but; in that moment he trusted me with his life, and to be quite candid, he trusted me with his wife's life too. We laid there and talked for a little while and then the caressing started again. Needless to say we went another round and his "snatch bar" didn't work the second time either. OF COURSE it was lingering in the back of my mind because there are just certain risks that you shouldn't take as a married man/woman. I believed that there were rules of engagement as it related to infidelity. The cardinal rule was that the other woman should never get more time, money, attention, or dick (especially raw) than your wife. Pillow talk and overnight stays when you live no more than twenty minutes apart is unacceptable and giving your side chick access to your wife are both major NO-NOs. After the second time, we talked for a couple of hours while we spooned. I knew that I wasn't the first woman that he stepped out with and I knew that he understood the risk he was taking, but; I also knew that he didn't understand that the risk with me was far worse than the return was. What he did understand was that I was the intimacy that he needed during that time. He and I yearned for one another and while I wanted him more than I wanted food, I had to remember that he was unavailable. For more than three years, DP and I would flirt with the idea of seeing one another. I'd get a random message that she was going to be away so "that mean we could play house." As much as I loved our intimacy, I kept us safe because I knew what was good for him and it wasn't me. DP was my first married man and the beginning of a shameful season of killing the spirits of married men.

I have always been easy to talk to and my smile invites total strangers into my personal space daily. After leaving the gym one evening, I walked into a brand new local restaurant to grab a bite to eat. While waiting for my food, this gentleman kept smiling at me and began to make small talk. I engaged until they called my name, I got my food and as I began to walk away, a clean cut brother said, "excuse me" and handed me a business card. When he handed me the card, he said "feel free to call me anytime." I thanked him and walked out. Later that evening, I called the out of state cell number and held a very interesting conversation with him. I discovered that he was the owner of this major franchised restaurant and I also discovered that he was a married man. Our conversations were always so interesting that sometimes he would sit in front of his community and avoid going home just to stay on the phone with me. For months, we would exchange text messages, pictures, FaceTime and hold phone conversations. We never had sex. What I realized was that he needed something from me that was deeper than sex. Sometimes a man just needs a woman who will listen, speak truth, and deflate his fears when necessary. Everything was okay between us until the day his wife read his text messages. After that day, he kept in contact, but; our friendship changed significantly. I explained to him that his marriage, business and family were his priority and we stopped communicating cold turkey. Moving forward, often times when I saw him we would exchange silent words and other times he'd sit and talk to me while making rounds through the restaurant.

Then there was a man that I met as a government contractor. I was primarily responsible for inviting attendees to a security symposium. This particular invitee was an attractive, dark chocolate brother who stood 6'2" and was built solid with a nice body (for a brother in his 50s.) He had the deepest voice and a posture that would intimidate another businessman. He literally had my attention from the moment that he said hello. When the symposium was over, he left immediately afterwards. Before he did, he got my contact information from one of his colleagues who was a CEO/Owner of a security company that contracted to the agency that I worked for. He didn't waste time calling me and I didn't waste time engaging. Chuck and I carried on a relationship for four years off and on. He owned and operated a weapons training company and kept crazy hours, so he was available whenever I needed him to be, but; never for as long as I wanted him to be. There were nights that he would come in, make love to me, wash up and leave. Then there were days when he would come, sit and talk for a while, take care of me and then leave. We had a relationship with defined boundaries and I was okay with it until a warm day in May when he pressured me into giving him some "loving." Before he came to my house this particular day, I told him that I didn't want to have sex, but; he just wouldn't take no for an answer. He was extremely aggressive and passionate and it scared me because I had never seen this side of him before. He threw me down on the couch and yanked my pants down. As he stroked me with his hand and began to gently slide his fingers inside of me, he used his other hand to unbuckle his pants. He pulled out his penis and slid it inside me. After less than two minutes, it was over. He ejaculated inside of me and I was angry. Not because it ended so quickly because I was used to five minutes of fun, but; I was upset because he came inside of me. He was a healthy brother and had multiple children so I knew he could produce children. My anger quickly turned into fear. A little more than a month later, we were pregnant and he was scared. I had access to his wife, home address, business partners, etc. Our easy relationship became easily complicated. Not only were we pregnant, but; it was multiples. This was my third time being pregnant with multiples and this was going to be the hardest abortion of them all. After having the abortion, Chuck was as supportive as he could be but the dynamics of our friendship was greatly impacted. However; our friendship was stronger than it was before. Although that was the last time we made love, it wasn't the last time we connected. He was later deployed on a special operations mission in another country and we would FaceTime every morning before he went to work and every night before he went to bed. We shared a bond that shifted from sex to security. I had to walk away because we were too dependent on one another and loving him was too easy. Chuck was different from the rest and after our experience, I recall waking up one day asking myself, "Tamika, do you want easy or do you want everlasting?" That was the day that I decided that my days of being with someone else's husband was over. I desired more than temporary satisfaction. I was ready for everlasting fulfillment!

What I realized is that just because a man wants to have sex with you doesn't mean that he loves you. Just because he sneaks away from his wife and family to be in your bed for a couple of hours, doesn't mean that he is choosing you over his wife. It means that you're convenient, readily available, and a moment that he may or may not remember. That's not love. Its infidelity and it comes with a significant price. I'm confident that he won't volunteer to pay the price for you, so think twice before you entertain someone else's husband. I was her once upon a time, BUT; I will never be her again. Let's be clear! I'm not endorsing or promoting infidelity in any way. I just view it differently from others, especially having been on both ends of the spectrum. Infidelity may be the end of a marriage, but; it's not the end of the world. Anything that exploits, demeans or destroys is not of God. I believe that God meant for marriage to be eternal. So, when you choose your husband or wife, make sure you choose with your mind because you will consider him or her in every choice you make. Most importantly, make sure you choose with your heart. Love is a sacrifice and constant change. Therefore, you must be prepared to love your spouse even when you feel rejected. You must also be willing to learn your spouse every day because their yesterday is not going to be their today.

I believe that marriage is a cycle of life and I also believe that it's the divine power of God that puts people together or the desperation of one's flesh. This will ultimately determine the substance and success of the marriage.

"Be in love with the covenant NOT the man!"

Eliminate Sex from the Equation

"Believing in love is the most important thing that one will ever do, just never confuse love with lust."

With anything you do there is a process and I've been going through a rigorous dating process for the last ten years. What I realized in my early thirties is that nothing is going to happen until it's time. I have always chosen my mates and most of these relationships were based on sex because I felt like I wasn't in need of love. You should never mix love with lust. I knew that for men, sex is mental and they have to think of something before they're aroused, but; for women, sex is emotional. They have to feel something before they're excited. For example, I was making love to my partner and after a minute I asked him, "who have you been with besides me" and as he slowed down his stroke became more intense (which to me meant that I reminded him of the way she felt inside). I began to feel the way that he stroked her in that very moment. He quietly replied, "no" and moaned (which was normal). I placed my hands on his chest, pushed him back, and said, "Yes you have because your stroke is different." Then his stroke became even more intense, which was his way of trying to create a diversion and he said "Mika, I enjoy your pussy too much to worry about another woman." I looked him in his eyes and softly said to him, "it's ok Baby because someone else has been in this pussy that you enjoy so much so you keep fucking her and I'll continue to feed him your pussy." Instantly, he lost his erection. I wasn't expecting to climax with him because I had never cum during penetration with him. However; I wanted to continue because whatever he thought about when his stroke became more intense felt good and so did sharing my truth.

Please understand that a man will never be able to accept another man penetrating what he THINKS is his vagina even when there is no defined commitment. That's like a man eating a burger that's absolutely delicious and then him leaning over and allowing another man to enjoy the rest of his burger. I was never a fan of sharing, especially if he was good, but; if there was no defined commitment then we were both fair game. You have to meet people where they are, so if he's not ready for a commitment, don't expect to change his mind. Accept where he is or don't bother wasting your time. "Over stand" that he is a man and they generally take what they want and keep it moving. If he comes back, three times, then he's confirmed that he enjoys what you do for him physically. I don't believe that men get attached to great sex; I think they just appreciate or take advantage of the fact that we are naive enough to keep allowing them to use us for great sexual encounters. I believe when men can't get the same thing out of you that they are accustomed to getting it will change the dynamics of your relationship. I also believe that when men stop getting what they want from you, they move on to the next woman who's willing to give him what he wants.

After ten years of sleeping with men and giving them my soul night after night, I still felt empty and insignificant. I thought to myself, "what is really of value to me and why do I feel depleted and empty?" I decided at thirty-three that I wanted a relationship of substance, but; I still kept choosing all the wrong men for all of the wrong reasons. I remember listening to a Pastor say "You can do one of two things. Obey me and prosper or do it your way and remain stuck." This hit home because I've spent the vast majority of my adulthood rushing through life, skipping steps, missing opportunities in the process and staying stuck. When you feel like you're stuck, it's difficult to watch other people move on and that's when it becomes complicated. I began to doubt my ability to choose the right man and I started to tell myself that sin feels good and doing the right thing feels uncomfortable at times. I also began to tell myself "when in doubt, don't do it." I wanted to know that a man wanted more from me than a good time. For once, I wanted my heart to choose, not my womb.

I recall meeting a man that I'll just call "Wink." We met through social media, which I had never done before at that time. We began talking for hours on FaceTime and on the phone. He was single, no children, handsome (even having a prosthetic eye) and he didn't care that I was a single mom of five because he liked children. He definitely wasn't the man that I would generally go for. He was seven years my junior, he had just come home from doing ten years in jail for murder and practically became a man while in prison. That concerned me because I believe that some men who are institutionalized have a difficult time re-adjusting to society as men and I was raising three young men who needed someone who was capable of covering, protecting and providing for them when that time came. We started spending a substantial amount of time together and eventually I introduced him to my children. After spending a couple of months around one another just about every day, he decided that he didn't want to share me. I asked Wink "what are we were doing because

I've played house before and I'm not interested in doing that again?' He replied and said, "Mika, I don't want to be with anyone but you!" Shortly before that, we held a lengthy conversation, while we were lying in bed, watching TV and talking about everything BUT sex. What I loved about our relationship was that he and I eliminated sex from the equation and it proved to be the best relationship I had with a man over the course of the last five years. We learned so much about one another. He became my youngest daughters Godfather and he would participate in school conferences. He would pick my youngest son up from school when I was sick. To be quite real, he did more for four of my children than their biological fathers had done for them since birth. Eliminating sex enabled us to view one another with a renewed mind. He admitted that I was the first woman that he had to open a door for. Yes, he said "HAD to" because I didn't settle for anything less. He honored me, he respected me, he loved me, and he catered to me. Most importantly, I had finally realized that self-control wasn't as difficult as I thought it was and I was honoring God for once! I had found what I love and wanted to keep him around for as long as I could. He became an ex-boyfriend, but; family for a lifetime. My relationship with Wink was the one and ONLY relationship where I tested my mother's theory and I learned so much about men BUT most importantly, I learned so much about myself. I still wasn't ready for a serious commitment with him so I found a way out without hurting him. There will come a point in time when some of your strongest relationships and bonds are tested. During this time, you will be able to differentiate seasonal friends and superficial bonds from the relationships of substance. Wink was a relationship of substance and when I felt like we learned what we needed to learn from one another, I moved on.

I am a female version of him

**"Men seldom commit in the spiritual when
they've been operating in the natural."**

Growing up I watched the men in my life and I paid close attention to how they treated the women in theirs. I witnessed some of
them effortlessly run major game on women and I learned a great deal.
I watched my dad take full advantage of women financially, mentally,
emotionally and physically. I learned all I needed to know and by the
time I was old enough to date, I was heavily guarded and ready to play
games myself. I spent a great deal of my time around men who "played
women," which is why I knew what "game" looked like. My mother
slept with a man (my biological father) who spent the vast majority of
his life creating opportunities where women took care of him with my
mother being "the exception to the rule." I used to tell people that
instead of killing the enemy, my mother slept with him. They created
me and that combination would prove to be the beginning of something beautiful, lethal and life altering for many brothers who caught
the backlash from a woman who knew exactly what they were capable
of. Let me be clear that not all brothers that I encountered were like
my father and not all of them came with game or an agenda. I truly
believe that the way you behave is a reflection of what you believe.

As a result of my preconceived notion that all men were dogs,
the innocent became victims of my shenanigans and my guarded

heart. Regardless of what they professed, proclaimed or confessed, the minute I felt as if their words and actions weren't in alignment, the manipulative and vindictive beast in me would rise. Outside of watching men like my biological father, who had a wife and "multiple girlfriends" (at the same time), I also watched my mother (who was my role model) posture herself in a way that commanded respect from men over the years. Although she sheltered us from many storms and she didn't expose us to the adult "issues" that occurred between her and her male companion, husband or significant other, we saw enough to know that "Momma didn't play any games." She didn't tolerate much and to be quite honest, I witnessed men get the axe because of her zero tolerance for non-sense. I'm sure she didn't just give up, but; she also didn't allow any of them to use her as a punching bag, doormat or as a bed warmer.

I didn't just get my game from the men in my family and from watching my mother. Three of my best friends are strong African-American men whose only weaknesses were beautiful women, quick money, fast cars or fashion. Needless to say, over the years I learned a great deal from them as well. Life is filled with lessons, which facilitates growth. There's always an opportunity to learn something from someone. I don't know anyone who has all of the answers, but; I consistently stayed connected to those who I felt could supply me with what I needed to stay sharp and informed. I dated one of my male best friends in my late twenties. I remember shortly after we got pregnant, he tried to play with me. The minute I peeped his game not only did I call him out on it but; I immediately severed all ties. He was shocked and spent months begging for my forgiveness. When I finally allowed him back into my life, he told me that he knew better from the beginning but he had to try his hand. I thought to myself, heck, most men do. To this day, we have a beautiful bond and it's strictly platonic between us. He calls me for advice and to run scenarios past me before he tries it.

When a woman has confidence, it dictates how she behaves in the presence of men, but; especially in the presence of other women. As a woman I found that often times we (as women) subconsciously compete with other women who have no idea that we even exist. Men can see that there's a competition and he's going for the woman who appears to dominate. I never tried to compete because I've always commanded attention from both men and women. I dominated women who were obviously competing for attention because while she was focused on beating me to him, I was already catering to him. Although the men were fully aware of the game that was being played, I refused to show them my hand. I believe that you have to stay three steps ahead of men because when they move it is methodically. Therefore; you should be prepared to move when he moves. I walked into every situation thinking to myself that every man who under estimated me was positioning himself in an uncomfortable space.

Back then I was fully capable of reading men and I had the ability to see and get what I wanted without opening my legs. I also had the ability to block those people and things that were hazardous to and for me. But; as I lusted more and more, "My GREED" began to overpower my ability to read them and that's when I became incapable of guarding my heart. If I didn't want to know the man I was sleeping with I turned off my ability to read them. As women we have the ability to preserve everything and poison anything to include men. Shortly after losing my sister and divorcing my ex-husband, I decided that "life was too short" and although it was such a cliché term, I found it to be true. I decided that I was going to enjoy every moment as if it were my last. In life, you only get one opportunity to make a first impression and that first impression will govern the direction of the relationship from that moment forward. Initially men would get fun, firm, stable, and responsible and loving from me. I was extremely accommodating when it came to their needs or at least I made them believe I was. As I matured, I came to the realization that a man is generally concerned about a woman's appearance and what she's capable of doing for him sexually versus what she does for his soul. So, for more than a decade, I played on the fact that men were generally "weak" for the wrong woman with the right skill set. They would pay my bills even while I had a man living with me. One brother in particular would pay daycare, buy gifts and always provided me with a monthly monetary stipend for nearly two years. I would feed their egos, make them hunger and thirst for more (of me). Then I would intentionally destroy what they believed was the perfect situation when the relationship was no longer beneficial to me. I would ruin lives and leave men to carry the emotional baggage from the dissolved relationship and I didn't have any remorse. For more than a decade, I toyed with men and I didn't care that they didn't like being emasculated.

Eventually, I realized that regardless of how compassionate, loving, nurturing and positive I could be there was a side of me that became desensitized to men. As a result, I totally disregarded the fact that all men weren't the same.

My WOMB chose him, and him and him!

"Strip a man of his ability to choose and he will lose his power."

*I*n some cultures, a woman's worth and value is often times predicated on how many children she can bare. In other cultures, it's based on what she can do to please a man and that's where many of my victims made their mistake. They thought they were choosing me, but; my womb chose them!

In my opinion, "Womb Choice" is when your body says yes to a man before you do because there is something he possesses that your body needs. I first learned about "Womb Choice" from my sister/cousin, who I'll call Queen! While I was getting my lashes done one day, Queen and I were talking about men and after she listened to me talk about my sexual chemistry and energy, she began to educate me on "JuJu Mama" and the concept of "Womb Choice." As Queen continued to talk to me in that calming tone, it all began to make perfect sense to me. Like Queen and my cousin Tarsha, I have always attracted people, especially men, regardless of what I looked like on any given day. Plenty of people know us, some may never understand us, but; many will want to experience us. What's interesting is that we are all Libras and we all possess this undeniable ENERGY that most people (both women and men) want to feel and connect with. This type of energy is called "JuJu." It's a term used to describe "magic," which is something you should feel and not see. We as women should possess a natural ability to create opportunities and to develop relationships that will be equally beneficial. Unfortunately, some women don't understand this, so they just live in a comfort zone and miss opportunities. I used to be one of those women until I gained a thorough understanding of the magic that I possessed. I realized that I was filled with "JuJu" but; because I had been over selling myself and investing in all the wrong men for more than a decade, I forfeited my right to any residual I would've seen. It was as if people felt the "magic" in me, but; I didn't feel it, so I missed out on opportunity-after-opportunity.

I have a gift, but; didn't discover that until I was in my mid-twenties. Although I knew I had a gift, I didn't know exactly what that gift was until my late-twenties. When I was twenty-nine years old, I discovered that I had the gift of influence. I used my gift to my advantage in my early twenties and didn't realize that's what I was doing. The gift of influence is one of many gifts that GOD blessed me with. Until I was twenty-nine, I didn't understand that I had the ability to make someone do something and make them think it was their idea, especially men. To some men, making them do what I wanted them to do was me play-ing mind games. To me, it was called creative manipulation and it was because of "Womb Choice." I needed them for one reason or another so I learned how to transfer energy, both negative and positive over the years. There were times when I would meet a brother, make eye contact and if my womb decided it needed him, I would then have him. No questions asked. Just an equal exchange of energy. Over the years, I discovered that I have what has been referred to me by men as a sexual gift and I almost always used it to manipulate men to get what I wanted. I've always been a big flirt, but; as I matured and came into who "I am," I learned when and how to use my sexual gift.

There are women who have lived vicariously through me. I be-lieve it's because I am a woman who is extremely confident, secure and sure of both me and my capabilities as it relates to just about every aspect of life. Making and keeping a man happy whether it's feeding him mentally, spiritually, emotionally or sexually came natural. Before I understood my gift and how to utilize it, sex was just a blinder for me. During that period, I could only connect with a man sexually. If his sex was amazing, my criteria and standards became an option and having him inside of me then became the priority. If his sex was weak, I was on to my next partner. Sex also became a tool for me and there's nothing more dangerous than having tools and knowing exactly how to use them.

Every man has experienced that moment when he woke up with her on his mind. That woman that does something for his mind, body and/ or soul. That one thing that is indescribable. I knew when my men experienced those moments because I'd get that 3 A.M. text, call, or video call. Some of you are thinking that it's just about sex, but; OF COURSE it's so much deeper than sex. Often times, those calls didn't end in a night of bumping and grinding. There were nights when that 3 A.M. phone call turned into a three- hour spiritual conversation that ended in tears. Then there were nights that those calls ended in a night of cuddling and talking about his fears, goals, dreams and plans. I was always consistent with each of them even when they were in rotation because I always wanted to be upfront about my intentions and expectations.

There were also men who my womb chose and they disappointed me, overwhelmed me or pushed me away because they wanted to recreate moments while I was interested in creating memories. I've experienced "Womb Choice" several times and I gave my body just what it wanted in that moment. You do have to be cautious about who you share your energy with because there are those who can be toxic for you.

My discernment was so on-point, but "Womb Choice" introduced me to one of the most complex experiences of them all. It was a man that

I'll refer to as "Coach!" The moment I saw him, I knew that I wanted him because my womb began to contract. He worked on Capitol Hill during the day and coached in the evenings. I quickly became addicted to him. What's unfortunate is that an addiction is something that stays with you for the remainder of your life if you're not careful. There was a small part of me that needed him for years. He was everything I thought he would be sexually and we had amazing chemistry. Most importantly, we had some of the most inspiring and motivating conversations. He CONSISTENTLY attended to my needs and desires, regardless of whether they were minor or major. We fed one another and there was always an equal exchange of energy. We explored one another and catered to one another until I got pregnant with my third set of twins, which is when our friendship really got complicated. He was angry and I was scared. Although we aborted and went our separate ways for a while, energy just kept pulling us together because he was weak for me and I enjoyed controlling him.

My second complex "Womb Choice" is a man that I've never met in person. He challenges me to think, meditate and he awakens the "juju" inside of me. From the very first time that we spoke, he inspired me to take my time, think, process, and respond to him with words of substance. His posture, which is a way of dealing with life, an attitude, or ones' approach to various situations, is that of a King. He understands how to bridge the gap between what's said and left unsaid. He understands that it's ok to be himself (FLAWS included) and how to embrace his journey. I had to learn the hard way and although my womb chooses, I have learned self-control and I've had to deprive my body of what it wanted because I realized that the need is so much greater than the desire.

The One HE Kept From ME

"Your most intimate prayer is silent and in the presence of other people."

I believe that it's difficult to embrace a good man, after you've already given your soul to more than forty bad men. I feel like I spent my entire life disobeying God and giving myself to unworthy men. I laid down night-after-night with men who I knew weren't designed for me. I gave my soul to demon-after-demon with hopes that I'd find my mate eventually. Sounds crazy I know, but; for nearly a decade, I just wanted someone to help me with my bills, satisfy my sexual cravings and to protect my family when needed. Eventually, I got tired and prayed for a husband because 1 Corinthians 7:9 says "But if they cannot control themselves, they should marry, for it is better to marry than to burn with passion." I knew that I had difficulty keeping my legs and mouth closed, so I wanted a husband. I made an effort not to defile my bed any longer. Needless to say, the prayers of the righteous avail not the desires of the desperate. I became desperate and that desperation began to breed disobedience. I was praying and playing around at the same time. I slowed down tremendously, however; I hadn't stopped. I felt like praying for God to send me a good God fearing man was pointless. I would pray morning, noon and night for God to send me my "BOAZ," who was a man often times referred to as a "type of Jesus" by some Christians. Although this was my prayer, I knew that I wasn't ready and evidently, so did God.

One day, while in meditation, God said to me, "you're not just asking me; GOD; who knows all and sees all, to bless you with just any man, but; you're asking me for BOAZ." I began to cry because He was absolutely right. While I felt like I was ready for my King, I KNEW that I wasn't ready. I was broken, disgusted, overwhelmed with those demons that I had not asked to be cleansed of and I was a total mess. Men were my God because I was more concerned with being in their presence than I was with being in God's presence. I was living a self-righteous life in that particular season and had no idea what I needed because my only focus was on what I desired. A righteous woman deserves "BOAZ" who was the son of Rahab and Salmon and a wealthy land owner. According to biblical text, "BOAZ" was approached by Ruth and was asked to exercise his right and to marry her. I personally don't equate this to her getting down on one knee or asking a man to marry her. I equate it to a woman's ability to choose. I learned a long time ago that I am a chooser and promised God that I will chose accordingly when BOAZ presents himself.

This brings me to a beautiful day in October when I was driving down Route 5 heading home to pick my children up from school and to prepare for my birthday. The light turned yellow and as I was slowing down, I felt as if someone was watching me. When the light turned red, I came to a complete stop and as I looked to my right, there was a man just looking at me as if something was wrong. I said to myself "CREEP" and pulled up so that he couldn't see into my car. He then pulled up and I looked over again. He spoke and I waved and said "hi" (as if he could hear me through the window). He smiled and began to roll down his window. I guess that was my queue to roll my window down as well, so I did. He introduced himself as we exchanged smiles and had a brief dialogue in which case he asked if he could have my number. I gave it to him without any hesitation and about two minutes later, my phone rang and it was Russell. We began to talk and there was an immediate connection. We discovered so much about one another during that conversation and the most interesting thing was that we were both preparing to celebrate our birthday the very next day. The conversation was so beautiful that I didn't want it to end. I was instantaneously captivated by his energy, his light, and the positive vibes that he disseminated. The most attractive thing about him was the fact that he was so attentive to me. He preferred to see me in the natural. Ladies, please understand that, subconsciously, we dress, we emulate and we become what most men in our society considers status quo. Russell appreciated the total opposite and that drew me even closer to him.

Later that evening, I invited Russell over to visit. I felt so comfortable with him that I was not hesitant to allow him into my personal space. Of course some would think it's crazy to allow someone into your home that you've met less than ten hours prior. However; I'm different and I've always worked off of energy. Russell and I had the type of chemistry that you see in the movies. I also felt comfortable because I knew that my sister Tracy was coming by so we were not going to be alone. The entire evening that Russell was there we had an amazing time. My sister had a difficult time believing that we had just met that day because our chemistry was so strong and the energy was so positive. We were so comfortable with one another that it was a little scary.

We established an unwavering trust and the fact that we were both Libras told us about one another. In my opinion, Libra men and women are loyal to a fault, very genuine, nurturing, extremely compassionate, very protective, and at times we can be procrastinators. Listening to Russell was like listening to myself speak. I would always tell people that if you've never been with a Libra then you've never really loved. What I understood was that while Libras are great people, I know that a Libra man will take you on a whirlwind, blow your mind and then break your heart. Once you've gone too far, it's difficult not to keep going so I wanted more from Russell. Like myself, I believed that Russell had his own set of vices and worked diligently not to expose them. However,

I did something I had never done before. I walked into this friendship differently than I had with every man before him. I walked into our friendship trusting him, loving his existence, respecting him, and listening to the meditations of his heart. I walked into our friendship completely vulnerable.

Although our intentions were to honor God, one afternoon we allowed our flesh to overpower us. He and I began to make love and because we weren't ready, we stopped. Our intimacy was much deeper than penetration, and that's when I knew that he was definitely different. I enjoyed just being in his presence so sex wasn't a priority for me. Needless to say, we had a long conversation afterwards and it changed the dynamics of my feelings in that moment. I loved him even more than I had before and it had nothing to do with the act we committed, but; Russell's ability to regain self-control and his willingness to take full responsibility for what took place even though I was "the seducer." After that day, we waivered and had some of the most intimate discussions that led to tears, confessions and the sharing of secrets.

Approximately four months in, I finally decided it was time to ask God about Russell. I needed to understand why this time around felt so much different from the other time. I needed to understand why I was in love with a man and it had nothing to do with sex which was always my gauge. My prayer was so deep, so authentic and so heavy that it brought me to my knees in tears. God said to me "He is your husband, but; I won't allow you to make a mockery of your marriage as you have done others, so be still and wait as I prepare you both." I thought to myself, FINALLY, the man that I have waited for, a man that God has kept just for me, one that I can honor and serve. Even after a colorful past, I believe that marriage is sacred and should be treated as such. I chose not to stay in my first marriage because there's a distinct difference between an ordained marriage and a marriage. There is also a difference between you choosing him and him being chosen for you.

Over time, I battled with this answer because Russell and I had both started to see other people and I decided to settle in the "friend zone." I was famous for "dragging drama" from one relationship to another, which is what stopped me from evolving. I was used to failed relationships, but; this was different. When I discovered that Russell was seeing someone else, I simply said to him "be safe and let her know that she's seasonal because God promised me that you're my husband." My reality is that the soul wants what it wants and mine wanted HIM! His positive reinforcement and persona were the very things that drew me to him and the very thing that consistently calmed my spirit. I have benefited more from my relationship with Russell than I ever have with any other relationship. Heaven got a glimpse of who we were before it ever manifested on earth and knew exactly what we needed before we entered the world. God knew that I wanted every man I chose, BUT; He knew that I needed Russell.

What I've learned along this spiritual journey is that you must allow God to move how he desires so that you don't block your blessings. I also believe that when you fall in love, it is a reflection of your true values and a mirror image of who you are. I fell in love with the value of who I was when I fell in love with Russell. He represents who I am and I represent who he is. The most beautiful part of loving Russell is that we both represent GOD's love. When I found Russell I found the answer to my most intimate prayer, but; because I wasn't ready for him, God kept him from me and used him as preparation for the man that I deserve not the man I desire. What I do know is that for more than a decade, God has been preparing me for my BOAZ through the many failed relationships. Although He kept Russell from me, I will remain faithful because it's important to stand on a word that's been confirmed by God!"

The Friend Zone

Believe it or not, when a man truly loves you, he'll respect you more than you respect yourself. I have a few male best friends who have been in my life for a very long time and it's not because they had a vested interest in being a part of my life outside of the fact that they genuinely love me. Now, make no mistake about it, I have been in a relationship at some point or another with a couple of them, and I've even been pregnant by one of them. However; we realized that we were much more valuable to one another as friends.

"When you establish a bond that's measured by how deep he penetrates your heart versus your vagina, you have something worth protecting."

Don't Stroke His Ego

"Men now-a-days are like slaves; they need just enough to keep them satisfied."

The dating game today has become so complicated because of un-realistic expectations, the male and female ego, and lack of respect for old fashioned values. When it comes to men, I think that many of them are missing the blueprint thus lacking the spiritual, moral and emotional foundation needed to navigate through life. Because I recognize this, I proclaim that I'm raising some woman's dream not a nightmare. I'm teaching my sons that they are Kings by birthright and that a woman should only compliment who they are as men. I'm deter-mined to equip them with the tools they'll need to make it through life without having to rely on a woman to validate them as men. I believe that there's a myth that most women, especially full figured woman are insecure and need to be validated by a man in order to feel beautiful, valuable and wanted. When in reality, there's an overwhelming amount of men who are insecure and need to have their egos stroked in order to feel significant. During a conversation, a wise man once explained a theory to me which suggests that "men now-a-days are like slaves, they need just enough to keep them satisfied." He taught me never to give a man too much because some men don't deserve more than enough and that giving them just enough to satisfy them for the moment is all they need. He taught me how to enslave them for as long as I wanted to.

There were brothers who I had enslaved for years and truth be told, I still have control over several of them. All I have to do is make a call or send a text message and the toxic cycle starts over again because I gave them just enough to maintain control.

Before my friend taught me how to enslave brothers, I was a giver. As a giver, I became accustomed to investing everything into men. Big mistake! Although I was a giver and went above and beyond, I learned that some men were never satisfied. There was one brother that I'll call "Andre" who was handsome, educated, spiritual, established and a good communicator for the most part. He was everything that I desired in a man. There were only a few problems with him that had me constantly wondering if he was a good fit for me. Andre was pushing forty, single with no children and extremely spoiled. Although he was spoiled, I knew how to handle that. Andre and I enjoyed spending time with one another because it enabled us to learn more about one another and our intellectual conversations were interesting. After a few years of running, I decided to take things to another level. I still wasn't ready to go all the way with him, but I wanted to date and see where it could potentially go. Andre was the first time I tested the slave theory. I began to cook for him occasionally because I knew he was truly a bachelor. Then dinner turned into dinner and a "happy ending!" I would only do it occasionally because it was just enough to make him happy. Remember the idea was to make him happy, but; the goal was to enslave his mind. What I didn't bank on was that I was simply stroking his ego and creating a monster. See when you're cooking for a man who's not "your man," catering to his sexual desires and sharing intimate moments with him then your overdoing it. You're giving him way too much because it will boost his ego and create a sense of expectation within him. What I didn't know about him was while we were seeing one another he was self-righteous, so stroking his ego was dangerous. I first realized he was a self-righteous man while we were at dinner one evening. He was obviously intimidated by another man's presence and that's when I saw his ego rise. When a man feels threatened by another man's presence, his ego will emerge. I realized that I was feeding his ego.

My mother used to tell me that "the beast that grows is the one you feed the most!" A prime example of this is what I did to Dre. I fed him and his ego so much that he became ignorant. This is what happens when we, as women, lower our standards to accommodate the male ego. Because I gave him all of the amenities of a having me without expectation, I believe that he felt like he was my best option. This screenshot is of a conversation between Dre and I which solidifies his self-righteous, ignorance and misunderstanding of my worth.

I acknowledge that I played a significant part in creating this beast and while it's our responsibility as women to uplift our kings that does not mean feed their egos. What I believe is that most men don't understand that in the blink of an eye, everything that they have can be stripped from them and in that moment they become powerless. What's sad is that if you take a man's penis and wallet from him, he will immediately become inadequate. What's even sadder is that love has been removed from sex and intimacy in this culture.

A man needs something to motivate him and sometimes sex just isn't enough. He needs his ego stroked, he needs to feel important, and he wants to feel needed. I am the type of woman that could make any man feel like a king, regardless of his social, spiritual or economic status. I do understand that the enemy wants our Kings so we have to help men understand who they are, but; we can't handicap them in the process. It's my belief that we have been destroying men and tearing them down from the very beginning. Just think about this for a moment, Adam was convinced by Eve to sin. After he sinned, he immediately became dysfunctional and the cycle has since carried on.

Some women really believe that sex, cooking, kids, and love will keep a man's attention. When in reality, none of those things that we (as women) put value on will keep him focused. I don't care how good your sex game is or how great your cooking is, it's not enough to keep the attention of a "real man." A real man wants to know that you believe your value isn't predicated on what you can do for him sexually. He wants to know that you're capable of getting on your knees and going to God on his behalf. Now, inadequate men and insecure boys on the other hand are only concerned with whether you're willing to get on your knees to take care of them sexually and what you're capable of doing to boost their egos. They want to know what your bedroom skills are like and what you can do to make them feel adequate. The moment I realized that I was dealing with insecure men and boys, I got tired of getting on my knees and they became distant memories.

"Whistleblower"

"There should always be a connection between happiness and success. Most people develop a formula for success and fail at it because it's designed for self-gratification."

The "Whistleblower Protection Act of 1989," is a United States federal law that protects individuals who report agency misconduct, such as violations of laws, rules or regulations; blatant mismanagement; misappropriation of funding; an abuse of authority; or any action that poses danger to the health or safety to the public, while working or contracting to the federal government. This misconduct isn't limited to a past act. It can be an ongoing act or it can be something that's in the planning stages. If the federal agency makes an attempt to take retaliatory action against that "whistleblower," they are then in violation of the "Whistleblower Protection Act." This act protects employees from being fired or mistreated for blowing the whistle. During my tenure with the federal government as a contractor, I realized that I spent the vast majority of my career serving people, which is where I went wrong. Over a ten-year period, I witnessed things that you see unfold on dramatizations of a broken government. When I got fed up and was asked to break the law, I decided to blow the whistle. I was considered an "internal whistleblower" because I worked within the organization as a contractor. What would come after I blew the whistle forever changed my life and the way I view the government. Let's just say that they became desperate and that the retaliation was real, but; it backfired.

I began my career as a federal government contractor in 1998. During my tenure, I met some of the most amazing women who played a vital role in the success of my professional career. There was VeeLo, who was my Libra sister and fashion consultant. There was Leela, a woman who served as my professional voice of reason and account-ability partner. Then there was Di; an example of what I wanted to be in the future. I knew when Di stepped off the elevator because she possessed a distinctive walk that you could hear 200 feet away. She had what I called the "power walk." She was so smart and effortlessly commanded the attention of those around her. Amongst the managers, she was one of very few women and feared by the men. I believe they were intimidated by her so much that she was cheated out of a position that she was qualified for and that she "acted" in for more than a year. Lastly, there was Mrs. C, who was like a mother to me. She would often times give me recipes and share secrets that kept her marriage together for more than four decades. I loved my job and got to see how the government conducted good business practices. Unfortunately, when my company lost the contract, I was laid off and began to look for work. After six months of job hunting, I was offered a job to contract to at a federal law enforcement agency through a temporary agency, but; by that time, I was three months away from giving birth to my first child. I had to respectfully decline the position, but; as sure as GOD is good, I received a call the day after I gave birth to my daughter asking if I was still interested in the position. Their second selection didn't work out and the agency wanted to know if I was available. I accepted the offer, however; I explained to them that I wouldn't be available for the next four weeks. I went through the required clearance process and then I began contracting to the federal government again. This time would be drastically different from my previous contracting job. When I started contracting with this agency in 2003, we transitioned over to a newly formed government agency following the September 11th terror attack. When I initially started out, my job title was a Secretary IV, which came with a lot of responsibility and very little pay. I absolutely loved my job, especially when I discovered that my company had been under paying me more than seven dollars an hour for two consecutive years. I appreciated both the retroactive pay and the help from the federal employee who helped me to go after what was owed to me based on the US Department of Labor Wage Determination. I began to form relationships that are to this day very important to me. I learned from some of the smartest women and men that the world had to offer.

Like my experience at my previous government agency, I was happy, until I learned that the rumors of our broken government were true. I was a loyal employee who didn't mind doing the jobs that no one else wanted to do. I didn't care if it was sitting in on a teleconference for my Chief or making a lunch run for the Regional Director. I was so dedicated to my job that I worked up until the day before my labor was induced and returned to work just two weeks after each child (with the exception of one) because I was the only one serving in my position. I was also so dedicated that I did things like work more than twenty consecutive hours to clean up a mess created by those higher up, while my daughter slept on a conference room table. Thankfully, I had people there who genuinely cared about me like Jay, who went to McDonalds and bought my daughter some dinner while I worked to prepare for senior leadership to appear on Capitol Hill the next morning.

Although I loved my job, I was constantly stressed and overwhelmed. What I began to realize was that the stress I endured helped me to re-build daily. I became the dumping ground because I was the person that just about EVERYONE came to for everything. Over the years, I got tired of watching management demean and demoralize their subordinates. I was tired of employees being favored because they were having sex with their managers. I got tired of watching people claim twelve hours and they didn't work more than two hours. Needless to say, I became tired and the only thing I looked forward to was seeing my friends and helping clients.

My weariness became obvious during an all hands meeting when I felt compelled to speak up after my former supervisor, who I'll call "Twin" yelled and cursed at me during a phone call. To add insult, I was on speaker phone without my knowledge or consent, while others listened. This was evidence of the oppressed environment we were in where bullying was a daily ritual. I felt like it was unfair to be bullied by men who walked around carrying weapons. In the law-enforcement realm, training and supervision are the two things that determine the success of that agency or program. Our program was rapidly failing. My supervisors became more concerned with how many women they could sleep with versus securing federal facilities and paying their vendors in a timely manner.

Over the course of the nine years and eight consecutive months that I served this agency, I possessed a clear understanding of various programs and the critical elements that constituted their operational effectiveness. I thoroughly understood security contracts, the chain of authority, the statutory and regulatory framework of federal contracts and the Acquisition Process. I was primarily responsible for the establishment of Standard Operating Procedures to refine internal (Regional) processes on specific policies and procedures. During my tenure, I was privileged to sensitive information, corruption, and the blatant mismanagement of several programs. I became accustomed to putting the government before myself, my family and God until Friday, August 31, 2012 when I got tired. I was in the process of assisting with an audit of personnel files for security officers who were stationed at federal facilities. During the audit, I discovered that an armed security officer tested positive for both cocaine and marijuana during his pre-employment substance screening. Based on the contract, a negative substance screening was a pre-requisite for entering on duty on ALL contracts. I immediately scanned and copied the original forms and asked the project manager if the security officer was currently working. The Project Manager verified that the Security Officer was working and had been since he tested positive for illegal substances in 2008. Because I served as the regional expert in the assessment and proposal of monetary deductions, which was a mechanism used to impose monetary penalties against contractors for non-conformance with contractual obligations based on the Federal Acquisition Regular (FAR Part 52.212-4) for forty-six contracts and the implementation of disciplinary actions, I was responsible for assessing a deduction against the security company, which should've subsequently been returned to the respective federal agency. After discovering the aforementioned, I took the prescribed steps to inform the contracting officer, executive Leadership and the company. I immediately notified the contracting officer of the deficiency and began to process the assessment. The vice president of the company was my designated contact for this incident, which posed a problem because of his relationship with management.

On September 4, 2012, I received a call from the "Boss," while he was away after they got wind of my findings. The "Boss" asked me to "make the drug screening disappear." Boss told me that they didn't want it to show up in their performance appraisal (which is used to measure their performance for future contract opportunities). I was beyond disgusted at that point and immediately called my supervisor and informed him of the conversation and how uncomfortable it made me. When the "Boss" and his followers, specifically "O" found out that I moved forward and refused to participate in their unethical practices, they immediately retaliated against me. This didn't surprise me because I knew too much about their illegal business practices. They needed to silence me.

Weird things started to happen and I paid attention to every detail and kept a log of it all. The second in charge approached me and said, "I heard you wrote a lot of resumes for the new company, is that true?" I replied by saying, "yes" because I didn't see a problem with helping my co-workers considering I have written the resumes` of many of the government personnel to include The "Boss" and "O." I went on to tell them that I actually composed "O's" resume` from scratch and I applied for their PM-I Certifications. After we were done talking, I left for the day. I went out of town on that Wednesday and Thursday to attend a funeral in Greensboro, NC, and returned to work on Friday. By the time I had returned to work, all hell broke-loose and it appeared to be as a result of my findings.

After these series of events, they became more aggressive and on Tuesday, September 25, 2012, the contract staff from all sections to include myself were called into a mandatory meeting where we were informed by management that we were being extended on our contract for another 60 days because of "an incident that occurred so the contract was pushed back." I left that meeting and went back to my desk and began to document everything said in that meeting and combined it with the series of events. I was ten steps ahead of ALL of them. On Thursday, September 27, 2012, I arrived to work as I normally would. I entered the garage with no problems, I accessed all of the access controlled doors without any issues and I went to my desk, but; when I tried logging into my computer, it said "Your accessed has been denied. Please contact your administrator." I called the Helpdesk who informed me that my computer access was denied and had to be reinstated internally. I had never missed any IT Awareness Trainings and my clearance was active so I knew my denied access was not a result of training nor had I done anything that warranted it. I was told by Helpdesk to go to my ITFO Administrator, so I went to the office of the ITFO's Supervisor and knocked on the door, she said "come in." As I was walking in she made reference to "people being escorted out." She was behind closed doors with our Chief and "O" (all of which were on the Technical Evaluation Board for our contract.) I explained to her the problem I was having and she said, "I'll look into it." I said, "thanks" and closed the door. I went back to my desk and after sitting and thinking, I decided to call my company because from the day I refused to destroy evidence for "The Boss" and the day I turned a letter over that prompted a visit from the Office of the Inspector General (OIG), it became a very uncomfortable and hostile work environment. After talking to my company I waited. While in the hallway, I was instructed by ITFO's supervisor to ask "O" about my access. I sent an email from my BlackBerry about my access. "O" acted as if he had no knowledge that I didn't have access when he was in fact the person who initiated the act to deny me access. I was told by an Acting Commander that "Management was just trying to scare me and that I should just be cool and not call my company anymore." I shared with my company the many unethical practices, illegal behavior and harassment that occurred during this incident and prior. After talking to my company, I was instructed to leave the building and not talk to anyone on the way out. My Director, instructed me to call him once I left the garage. I contacted him and I also called OIG and scheduled an appointment just as my good girlfriend Lola had done days prior.

Once I turned over my blackberry, badge and left that building, The "Boss" became so desperate that he had another supervisor call me and try to come to my home to talk to me. When the phone rang, I knew what he wanted so I asked her who asked her to call me and she confirmed that the "Boss" did because he wanted her to talk to me. I respectfully declined and told her to stay out of it. I told her to tell them, "I'm going to do to them what they did to me after nearly ten years of service, and that was give them my ass to kiss." I meant that and it's exactly what I did. Their many attempts to scare me into silence didn't work. I went in for my interview and just thirty-five minutes into my interview, I suggested that they go get my belongings because there was a habit of hiding their secrets and keeping people quiet through fear and intimidation. I also told them about "O" having my computer access denied for absolutely no reason other than to scare me. ALL of my belongings to include my computer, blackberry, and eighteen boxes of stuff were seized while I was in their office. I was interviewed for six consecutive hours and we discussed the mismanagement, the harassment, and the unethical and criminal behavior. I turned over everything to include my training certificates to support the unlawful access denial. I shared the many unethical and criminal behaviors that occurred during my tenure such as the misappropriation of funding, the budget section purposely overbilling other federal agencies, and the purchasing of TVs with government credit cards (a few of which were taken to their private residences). I also informed them of how they hid millions of dollars to pay for excessive overtime. I shared that senior leadership made me write performance appraisal reviews for government employees although I wasn't a rating official. Based on a Directive, it's unlawful for anyone other than a rating official to do what I had been doing for several years. The disgusting behavior went beyond illegal behavior. The managers were sleeping with employees. The "Boss" had his executive assistant take his online college classes for him and in return was paid in overtime until they opened a federal position that they pre-selected her for.

What was frustrating was that we would deduct money, but; they never returned it to the federal agencies that it belonged to. They improperly stored records and files. They didn't conduct market value research, perhaps it's because they didn't really know how to do this. "O" had a contractor taking his online training for him which was unlawful. What baffled me was that this group of police officers committed more crimes than they made arrests. I remained loyal to them until they tried to force me to break the law. It was bad enough that they made me do things like answer congressional inquiries even after a Directive prohibiting contractors from answering congressional inquiries was disseminated. I trained auditors on how to audit their records and we went through my belongings and pulled out all the evidence they needed.

Since "O" was messy, he sent my company a request to remove me from the contract after they found out that I blew the whistle. This was clearly retaliation. They tried to use my attendance, but; the contracting officer for the agency declined their request to remove me and instructed my company to keep charging eight hours for every day that I was off. I saw e-mails where "Twin" stated that they needed to find something to get rid of me which was another attempt to retaliate. Field investigations began and the entire management staff to include "The Boss," "O" and "Twin" went back to their original positions and were replaced with suitable managers. The egregious and blatant disregard for the law, unethical standards and unbecoming behavior of people who were supposed to uphold the laws are all examples of this broken government that we have.

"Integrity is about doing what's expected without being asked to."

The Valley

**"Who shall separate us from the love of Christ?
Shall tribulation, or distress, or persecution, or
famine, or nakedness, or peril, or sword?"**
ROMANS 8:35

It troubles my spirit when spiritual folks pick and choose the parts of the Bible that they want to use as a sword. They'll take a book written to feed the spirit and paraphrase verses to circumvent reality, spiritual law and their wrong doings. Of all the things that I've done, I have not used scripture to justify my unacceptable behavior, but; I have used scripture to guard my heart, thoughts and mind.

According to the dictionary, the valley is defined as "a low area of land between hills or mountains, typically with a river or stream flowing through it." The valley is also defined as "a depression or hollow resembling or suggesting a valley, as the point at which the two slopes of a roof meet." In the spiritual realm, the "Valley" is often times referred to as a dark place. A place lacking protection or a dry place. Life is filled with valleys and nothing will ever be able to prepare you for those valleys.

What I learned is that God wants you to come to Him in the most uncomfortable state. He wants you when you no longer have the answers. He wants you to come to Him when you're ready to surrender everything that is comfortable and familiar. Those things that keep you in bondage are generally those things that you become comfortable with. I realized that when I became comfortable with something, I then became lazy and I stopped fighting. Until the day I woke up and realized that the only way that the enemy wins is if I stopped fighting. I decided to be silent and to be still because although I was in the "Valley," God saw fit to save me after all that I had done. Therefore, I was committed to traveling through this journey called life fearlessly with both faith and a humble spirit.

In 2007, I visited various churches because I had friends who worshipped regularly and invited me to their churches. Worshiping regularly was something that I wasn't familiar with at first. I enjoyed those experiences, yet I never became hungry or thirsty until I accepted an invitation to a church in Clinton, MD. After having visited more than five churches, I had finally experienced the fullness of God and the presence of The Holy Spirit at the same time. I looked at the Pastor and said to myself this shepherd knows Jesus! Not that the Pastors before him didn't, but; there was a light in him that I hadn't seen before. I developed a hunger and a thirst for knowledge and understanding of God, Jesus, and the Word of God. I began to attend regularly, although I still had one foot in the word and one in the world, I was fighting daily to live right and to serve God. Every Sunday, I felt like the Pastor was preaching to me or about me. Perhaps it was because I was consistently compromising my salvation. It wasn't until 2009, shortly after I had given birth to my fourth child (Messiah), that I decided to answer that tugging at my heart to choose this as my church home. As I was walking to my normal seat, I was approached by Ms. J, who was the wife of my co-worker that invited me to visit the church two years prior. She said to me, "Are you ready to take that walk today?" I replied by saying, "I'm going to join after church." Ms. J said "I'll walk with you." At that moment, God said to me "all you have is now and this moment." I decided to take Ms. J up on her offer. At the end of service during altar call, Ms. J walked up to me and grabbed my hand. She walked me down to the altar and then she hugged me and kissed me on my cheek. This public spiritual commitment to Jesus Christ was my profession that I was finally ready to stop hindering my relationship with God and my prayers. I never worshipped with false pretenses, however; I did experience spiritual warfare at times.

After joining my church, I endured a flood of emotions and experiences that prepared me for some of the most difficult seasons of my life. I spent nearly three years off-and-on in the valley where I was vulnerable and open for attack. It was in these seasons that the enemy had a clear view of me. Although I was attacked, I knew that the gift in giving my life to God and choosing Him was that I wouldn't die in the valley because there was favor over my life. I also understood that endurance is a spiritual weapon and it takes great faith to endure difficult seasons. I experienced failed relationships, I held on to people who were toxic to me, and I couldn't bring myself to forgive myself for things that I needed to let go of. I fornicated and had another baby out of wedlock, I slept with married men, I was promiscuous, and I persecuted others when provoked. My health began to fail and I experienced pain like never before. In these seasons, I became tired, oppressed, weary and frustrated, but; I still managed to smile on top of pain. I didn't understand that my decision to walk with Jesus Christ was a part of God's design to prepare me for the valley. I made a conscious decision to serve God and to walk BOLDLY in the anointing and authority that I was given. When you do something unconventional and BOLD, expect to get negative feedback and backlash because not everyone will understand your point of view and reasoning behind your actions. While in "The Valley" I decided to fast. Fasting is a spiritual discipline used to seek God's intervention and when combined with prayer GOD's mind blowing power is unleashed. "The

Valley" was noisy for me and when you have a lot of noise in your head; it intervenes with your ability to hear your own thoughts and GOD. Fasting was important to me because I believe that fasting also tames the noise in your head.

Before I began to fast and pray, I felt like I was dead. I believe that without Christ we are spiritually dead, which is like being physically dead. Death is often times defined as a spiritual separation. Without God we are "morally deficient" which causes us to do what we desire versus what God calls on us to do.

When problems arise and challenges present themselves in the midst of your journey to greatness, it's because Satan knows that God's plans for you goes beyond your wildest dreams. Satan's job is to position you where you feel like your heart has been snatched out of your chest and the ground no longer exist beneath your feet. Satan will make you believe your dreams are unattainable when in reality it's uncomfortable because you're preparing to birth a miracle. There's a King in you waiting to be birthed! Satan will trick you into a spontaneous abortion.

When you realize that something is broken in your life, you can either do one of two things. Fix it or avoid it until it breaks you. I've realized over the years that "before GOD can fix you, HE must first break you!" I was broken for sure and under restoration. For as long as I could remember, my flesh use to control me because self-gratification was my priority and not God. While in the valley, I got to a point where I learned to control it because serving God became my priority. I was tired of hurting and hiding my depression. In moments of desperation I learned not to be disobedient, and to be still and seek counsel from God not man.

I'm a controversial woman who knows first-hand that even the unclean and the immoral have value. However, you have to make a conscious decision to trust God and live to please Him and not man. When you do this, God will reverse the outcome of any situation, especially when He sees one of His children in despair. After I began to pray, praise and cry out, it unleashed power, prosperity, healing, hope, love, and peace. I had finally realized that the commitment of my heart dictated the outcome of my praises. When you live your life without God at the center of it, you forfeit your right to live a peaceful life.

"God has positioned you where you are in this very moment for a divine purpose. Remember that He can't take over until you let go!"

Mom of Multiples

> "Whenever a woman is in labor she has pain, because her hour has come; but when she gives birth to the child, she no longer remembers the anguish because of the joy that a child has been born into the world."
> JOHN 16:21

There is a distinct difference between mothering and reproductive choice. Mothering is when a woman takes care or her child or children. Reproductive choice is a woman's ability to have a baby using safe methods, the ability to refuse being sterilized and the ability to elect to abort if she so desires. Growing up I swore that I would never have children because although I loved babysitting everyone else's children, I didn't want any of my own. I was often times the designated babysitter for all of my cousins and because I got a glimpse of what it took to take care of a child, I decided mothering or reproductive choice wasn't for me.

When I became sexually active, I didn't always take the necessary precautions to prevent getting pregnant. I exercised "reproductive choice" and had my very first abortion in 1998 at the age of eighteen. After losing my virginity at fourteen, I didn't have sex again until I was sixteen, which was a horrible experience. I didn't have sex again after that until I met the "Dope Boy" a few months shy of my eighteenth birthday. We met while I was staying with my extended family in Southwest, DC. One day I walked to the corner store and there was one brother who stood out. I don't know what it was that made him stand out, but; he caught my attention! After weeks of seeing him and his attempts to talk to me, I finally took his number and a week later I called him. That first call was the beginning of a whirlwind relationship. He would take me with him when he went to do business which made me very uncomfortable, but; his time was limited so I took the time he had. After a few months of dating, we found out I was pregnant and things became complicated because he wanted the baby. I was on the fence because he was a "dope boy" and lived the fast life. After we found out I was pregnant, he became possessive and started to make demands. He would tell me things like I couldn't walk to the corner store because he didn't want any of his "runners" talking to me. Of course, I complied with his demands because I knew what he was capable of and I knew that he was indirectly involved in a few murders to include one that took place right behind my grandmother's building. I remember the last night I was with him. We made love and while we were lying in bed talking he calmly said, "You know I'd kill you if I find out you're talking to another nigga. As a matter of fact, don't even look at another nigga or I'll kill you." After I reassured him that he was all I wanted, he went to bed. I couldn't sleep. The next morning my mind was made up and the very next week, I decided to move back to Laurel, MD with my mother. I told him that I was just going back home to visit. Once I moved back, I told my sister, my keeper of secrets that I was pregnant and then I asked her to take me to have an abortion. I called him and told him over the phone that I decided not to keep the baby. He replied, "If you kill my baby, you better not ever come to southwest again because I'm going to do to you what you're doing to my baby." Needless to say, I aborted and that was the first and last time I knowingly dealt with a drug dealer.

Unfortunately, it wasn't the last time I chose to abort. Some people believe abortions are considered to be morally wrong. I believe that women should have a right to choose. I have thirteen "unnamed babies in Heaven" resulting from four abortions. A couple of these abortions were pregnancies of multiples and I battled with the abortions for years. The book of Proverbs (Chapters 4, 5 & 6) teaches us that there are six things that the Lord despises and seven that are an abomination. One of these is "hands that shed innocent blood." I was ashamed for years that I used abortions as a method of birth control. It wasn't until the "dope boy" contacted me eighteen years later after talking for four hours that I actually forgave myself for all of the lives that I took, especially the one he wanted so badly. Although I asked God for forgiveness and I apologized to him, I never forgave myself for what I had done. In fact, because I aborted my first baby two years prior to getting married, I believed that my miscarriages were punishment for the first "unnamed baby" that I aborted. For years I put that experience in the back of my mind.

Once I was married, I was ready to give my husband a baby. At twenty-four, I did just that. Prior to successfully giving birth to my first child, I suffered through five miscarriages. I remember crying every time I miscarried and being angry that I was having difficulty carrying a baby full term because there were women aborting and abusing children daily. What I didn't realize at that time is that God wasn't punishing me and He wasn't saying NO. He was simply saying NOT YET. What was amazing to me was that I lost five babies and God gave me back more than double of what I lost. I gave birth to five beautiful children who are my inspiration and the reason I started using the #MomOfMultiple hashtag on various social media platforms.

Each of my children represent an anointing that I possess sent forth by God. They all have a gift and a tendency to command love. To be in their presence is almost always a refreshing experience unless they're having a moment. My living children are the one aspect of my life that I wouldn't change even if I were offered millions of dollars and limitless power. Over the course of the last thirteen years, they have brought me unspeakable joy and they give me a will to live daily, a desire to become a better person, the patience needed to be a "Mom of Multiples," and an abundance of love. Being a single mom of multiples isn't an easy job and it requires hard work, consistency, sacrifice, constant change, and the heart of a lion at times.

I always tell people that my mother made being a "Mom of Multiples" look easy because she sheltered us from many storms. I decided to expose my children to parts of our struggle. I believe that children should get a real view of life so that when a storm comes, they know what to expect and how to persevere despite how difficult the situation may appear. Like anyone else, life had its peaks and valleys. When we had valley moments, I sat my children down and explained our situation to them. I always communicated with my children and answered the many questions they had. I've dealt with many adversities as a mom of five and each one has taught me a valuable lesson.

I learned to set my pride aside as I dealt with being displaced, sleeping in a comfortable chair for months, being evicted from my home, and even living without water and electricity. If it weren't for people like my Church family and a select few family members, and close friends, I don't know what I would've done. I recall my good girlfriend telling me to come to her if I needed anything. I was a mom who was used to doing it alone and taking care of others at the same time so accepting handouts wasn't a familiar space for me. Well I learned quickly to get out of my own way when I was living in a home with no water. I took her up on her offer to help me. When I reached out to her, she didn't think twice about writing me a check for the full amount of my water bill. As she handed me the check, she said, "take your children home, I've been in your position before and I know what it feels like."

Another lesson I learned was the importance of becoming an advocate. When my oldest daughter, Sekeme, was tested and diagnosed with a severe learning disability at the age of six, I had to become an advocate. Prior to being tested, her Kindergarten teacher recognized that Sekeme was having difficulties reading and volunteered to spend forty-five minutes each day after school helping Sekeme with her reading and comprehension. As she went through kindergarten, we discovered that she was a slow learner. Originally I didn't understand how it would affect her as time went on. I worked briefly with children who suffered with both mental and physical disabilities in my late teens. When I was growing up, children were called "retarded" when they learned different. I never believed for one minute that my daughter was "retarded." I always explained to her that she learned differently than her peers did. Children have gone from being classified as retarded or mentally retarded to "intellectually disabled." I had to go as far as filing a constituent complaint with my congresswoman to force the school system to provide my daughter with the services outlined in what's called an Individualized Education Plan. This was designed to assist her with educational growth. Answering congressional inquiries for nearly a decade equipped me with the knowledge and ability to advocate for my daughter.

Being a mother also taught me how to lead! I understood that they were always watching and that regardless of what is said, they emulate what they see before they repeat what they hear. Children need to believe in themselves and a higher power. I have been raising my children in the Baptist faith for the last eight consecutive years. I pour the love of God in them and I consistently instill the word of God in them. We live in a world where children are easily influenced by their peers and we as parents have to set standards and equip them with tools that are indestructible. We are living in a world where our children gauge their worth on how many likes they get on social sites.

While being a mom of multiples comes with a great deal of joy, it has also come with a great deal of tears, frustration, and sadness. Parenting comes with a multitude of responsibilities and requires an ability to supply mental, physical, emotional, financial and spiritual guidance. When I became a single mom, I knew that I couldn't fail at being a mom so I was committed to doing everything in my power to make certain that I set the "blueprint" for my daughters and my sons. I became devoted to training my sons to respect women and I became dedicated to training my daughters to respect themselves. Often times I found myself over-compensating for their father's absence and stressing myself out trying to make it happen on my own. There were days when I felt like I was failing as a mom because I couldn't provide them with everything that they wanted. There were even times when I struggled to provide them with what they needed. For instance, there were weeks when I didn't have enough money for haircuts, and I couldn't rely on their fathers so I grabbed my clippers, hair cape, comb and brush and I cut their hair myself. I stretched meals, I cried, I prayed, I yelled and I became overwhelmed with emotions more times than I care to count, but; I never gave up. I learned the true definition of the word sacrifice. I felt like I was giving up my desires, but; I was fulfilling a mandate placed on me. I was holding myself accountable for electing to have multiple children out of wedlock. The unfortunate reality of single parenting is we never intend for it to be that way. I trusted them with the most intimate piece of me as a woman and when the relationships failed, I was left to take care of the children BY MYSELF. Outside of being a God fearing woman, there's nothing I prize more than being a "**M**om **of M**ultiples!"

A wise man once said to me "Raise your children on your knees!" And I do just that.
#thewordsofCMC

Break the Cycle

When relationships fail, children should never be forced to carry the burden of that failed relationship. There should always be a UNITED FRONT for the children. This means that there's nothing that we (as parents) can't do together for the sake of our child or family. I learned this through watching my mother, step-father and my step-sister's mother as they learned to come together to co-parent without any negative energy or conflict. Of course it took lots of energy, hard work, respect and an emotional investment from all of them to make this work and it wasn't an overnight thing. As with any situation, there's going to be disagreements, resistance and adversity, but; at the end of a tough day, they were able to find unity in adversity. The fostered relationship between my step-sister's mother and my natural mother had become so special that they refer to one another as "wife-in-law" and I have always introduced my step-sister's mother as my step-mother (although she divorced my step-dad before I met her.) Their bond is so authentic that they get along more than they do with my step-dad and they've come together not just when they need to but when they want to as well. For instance, there have been times when my step-mom has called my mom and stopped over her house just to spend time with her and to talk with her. In January of 2015, my mom, step-dad and step-mom were all waiting with anticipation for the arrival of my step-sister's first son (King Zamir) who was being delivered by my favorite OBGYN. Our doctor understood the importance of support, so she allowed two people to go into the delivery room with my sister.

Needless to say, she chose to take both of her mothers in the delivery room with her.

Although I was raised in a two parent household, like any little girl, I would've preferred my "biological father" presence and attention. What I realized as I matured is that my "biological father" was in no condition to help raise me nor did he have any value to add to my life. In my opinion, for years, my biological father was the true definition of what some refer to as a "deadbeat dad," which is the voluntary absence of the father. My father's absence impacted me in a way that caused some deeply rooted issues which greatly affected me throughout my life, especially as a woman. I refer to these deeply rooted issues as "daddy issues." My "daddy issues" trickled over into my adult life causing me to make both temporary and permanent choices that would adversely impact my life in various ways.

Due to the prevalent absence of natural fathers and the deadbeat dad stigma, some fathers are not celebrated enough especially in the African-American community because of the phrase "deadbeat dad" and its association with the aforementioned community. I don't just celebrate fathers, I celebrate godfathers, step-fathers, uncles, mentors, and coaches who have assumed the role of a father figure. Regardless of their role as a father figure, they have elected to break the "deadbeat dad" stigma and that excites me! Real fathers are stand-up men who aren't afraid to "stand up." They're men who take care of their children and other children around them because they understand that relationships are not based on one's DNA, instead their relationships are based on love, bonds and emotional connections. What's interesting to me is that in today's society there are just as many absent mothers as there are fathers. At some point we need to "break the cycle."

In my opinion, there are only two types of fathers, those who rise to the occasion and those who run from responsibility. I know some of the greatest dads walking the earth today. Like My brother Ty, who is not just an awesome father to his three sons and one daughter, but; he also stands in the gaps for my three sons and two daughters. Then there's Mike. I acknowledge him as my dad because he assumed that role when I was ten years old and has consistently loved me and my children. Pop, as I call him, is my step-father and the reason that I was raised in a two parent household. He also played a vital role in my upbringing. Over the years, I've encountered men such as Wink, who became my daughters God-father after a brief courtship between us. Then there is a man that I absolutely admire as a father and mentor. I watched him parent, coach and mentor his son, who later passed away at the age of seventeen from cancer. The list of men who step up without making any excuses goes on-and-on.

Then there are those dads who step off for whatever reason leaving a child fatherless. As a mom of multiples, I knew that I had to parent with or without the support of their fathers. Unfortunately, I have five children who are fathered by four different men and only one of them stepped up from the day our son was born. Two of the fathers have been absent for the last three consecutive years and the other one has been absent since I was pregnant with our son. It's difficult because I need the physical, emotional and financial support to provide my children with all that they need. The most frustrating part is that men don't understand the negative impact that their absence has on their children. For instance, my son Rashard was tasked with writing a personal thesis where he had the option of choosing what he wanted to write about. He chose to write about his life and the title of his thesis was "Growing Up Without a Dad." As I sat and read it, my heart broke simply because nearly the entire paper was about ME. He talked about how much he admired me and that the absence of his father no longer bothered him because he didn't expect him to be a good father after his constant disappointments. There was one line that stood out while I was reading it. It read "The biggest day of my life was when I won my first championship game with the Silver Hill Bears. My dad promised that he would come and he never showed up, but, when I looked on the side line all I kept seeing was my mom who was also my "Team Mom." It didn't matter that he didn't come because he missed all eight games before. I was just thankful that my biggest cheerleader and number one supporter never left the sideline." At that very moment the tears kept coming and I cried out "Thank You Lord." It takes a lot of patience, courage and strength to parent but I can never replace his father. In fact, my only fear as a single mom is not being able to give my three sons the guidance that they can only get from a man. Thankfully, they have men like their uncles and football coaches who have stepped up and led without thinking twice about it.

This chapter isn't designed to bash fathers in any way. Instead, its purpose is to raise awareness of the impact of fatherless children, especially as it relates to young African American boys. Fathers need to understand that a child's spiritual foundation, education, emotional state, and their happiness is paramount to their success. I only pray that fathers find it within themselves to stand up and "break the cycle" just as Mike, Pop, Darius, Tyrone, Xavier, Uncle Van, Uncle Lester, Lil Lester, Kent Boone, Uncle Tommy, Martin and Barry Davis (just to name a few) have done.

Social Media

Social media has revolutionized the way we communicate with a massive number of people from all walks of life. It has dictated the way both men and women approach the opposite sex. I believe that it has also altered many of our views as it relates to our history, education, success, reality television, social acceptance, gender identification, spirituality, religion, intimacy, sex and love. It has increased our ability (whether committed or single) to resourcefully seek women and men or both in some cases using non-traditional methods. With the evolution of social media at our fingertips, both men and women have become bold in their efforts to make their fantasies a reality.

"Our History"

In my opinion, social media has diluted our history. Great deals of us have no idea where we come from, who we are, the struggle of our ancestors, or the history of those who controlled our ancestors. We also lack understanding of the evolutionary phases of slavery. Therefore, we consistently face many challenges and difficulty navigating through life understanding why some of our actions are unacceptable.

"Success"

I've witnessed social media destroy human beings from children being bullied and eventually committing suicide to celebrities being judged and allowing how they're viewed by society dictate the direction of their success. However, I have also witnessed some of my dearest friends become millionaires through taking full advantage of various social platforms.

"Reality Television"

Cheap imitations of what we see on reality television have become a representation of what our children desire to become. If what they see on television is their reality, then they are being set up for failure. The vast majority of what we see is scripted, edited, and provoked by what society craves. These drama filled shows that have become a guilty pleasure, even for me, are a distraction and are designed to enslave our minds. My mother always says that "it takes all types of people to make up a world," and reality TV exposes us to this harsh reality.

"Social Acceptance"

I believe that there's a generation of lost men and women who refuse to join hands, but; who desperately seek social acceptance from a culture that opens itself up to them. Social media has a way of controlling your brand, image, and your life even. Society dictates how women believe they should look, speak, dress, think and behave. I have noticed changes (some not so drastic and others that are significant) in the beauty ideals for women and men in my lifetime. I believe that women were always expected to maintain upkeep of their body and appearance. During different eras, women dressed and took on the appearance of those respective times and were respected more based on how they presented themselves. In today's society, women keep up their appearance and are judged based on how they represent themselves as women. So in that regard, beauty ideals haven't changed much, but; as it relates to social acceptance women make an aggressive effort to conform to society. Women have gone through and continue to go through drastic measures to make themselves more appealing through plastic surgery, living beyond their means to keep up with trends, and by compromising their health and lives to take on the looks of what's considered beautiful. They have continued to alter the way they look and the way they appear to both the opposite and same sex. During the course of my lifetime, I believe that a woman's beauty has determined the type of job she gets, the type of friends she attracts, and the husband she secures. Society has become huge on commodification, which is considered the process in which society turns a woman's body into an object used to sell a product or an item used to "refashion women's bodies." I believe that the efforts that we as women make such as wearing makeup, lingerie, body language and exposing body parts are segways into commodification, therefore; we dictate how we are viewed and used.

Social media today has significantly impacted the change in social acceptance. I believe that "social media" is the unstoppable force that has caused both women and men to desperately conform to what's socially acceptable. There is an unprecedented amount of pressure on women, both young and old, to conform to society's expectations just to fit into a "social class." Reinventing oneself has become necessary to get and keep the attention of others. I have never been one to conform to society because I'm a free spirit who lives outside of the box and I was born to stand out. When you live outside of the box there's going to come a point in time where you have to break ALL the rules to follow your dreams. I've never feared being ostracized because my preference is to be set apart from others.

I believe that "WE" as African Americans artistically own the music industry, but; have somehow allowed society to dictate how we express ourselves through the art of music. While some feel like they're freely expressing themselves, the harsh reality is that there is someone behind their brand pulling all the strings to keep them aligned with what's considered "socially safe."

"Gender Identification"

I honestly never considered the clear distinction between gender and sexuality. I was raised in a liberal household with a strong spiritual foundation. While I was taught to love everyone, I was also raised to believe that it was socially unacceptable for boys to act, talk or dress like girls. In my opinion, gender is the distinction between being male or female from a social or cultural stand point. Sexuality refers to the division of male or female and is based on one's sexual orientation. It is my belief that "gender" and "sexuality" overlap. The gender of a man or woman is generally based on social expectations. Where-as the sexuality of a man or woman is based on his or her biological sex. I believe that it is possible for a man or woman to be attracted to the same sex based on their gender and the opposite sex based on their sexual orientation.

"Spirituality and Religion"

I also believe that there is a clear distinction between spirituality and religion. The same way that I believe in the holy trinity. Everyone is free to embrace what they believe in. I live in a world where I am FREE to believe and worship who and what I want. I have a friend on one of the many social platforms I use who's a "non believer." He only believes in science. For him, facts only remain in the evidence tested in theory. He's definitely a controversial man, but; I love him because he provokes dialogue that we often times want to avoid having until tragedy strikes. I actually enjoy hearing his perspective on various topics and I agree with some of his ideals. I've seen people use the various social platforms to inspire, encourage, motivate, and pour into the lives of a massive number of people. On the other hand, I have watched how people use social media to turn people away from the church. So many people have a huge misconception about church, especially, the "Black Church."

"Intimacy and Sex"

After I got tired of looking at an inbox with more than two-thousand messages on one of the social sites I use daily, I decided to clean out my inbox. As I went through messages, I realized just how bold men are. I had more than two-hundred and fifty men approaching me over the course of a year. Either asking to get to know me, trying to take me out, or asking for a sexual encounter. Some were total strangers, while the vast majority of them were married, in committed relationships, engaged, ministering at local churches or were publically professing their undying love for their women just moments or days before they were in my inbox. One of these men was DP, the married man who I carried on a lustful relationship with. Social media has enabled men and women to consistently rekindle old flames they find through social media after years of not seeing them and risk it all for a few moments of fun.

"Love"

Love is a verb and by definition, it's "the state of deep affection, adoration and/or a state of being in love." In my opinion, love is an expression and is incapable of being partial to, weak or indecisive. Often times, I've found myself in situations where I had to ask people "what love looks like to them." We live in a society where people feel like you have to love them the same way that they love you which is insane to me. While there is an expectation of reciprocity as it relates to love, I believe that one will love the way that they know how to love. Some men feel like providing for their family is equivalent to loving them. Love of substance comes in the purest form and that is from the heart of an individual because it's not a thought, it's an act. I always ask people what love looks like to them because I'm always interested in hearing their responses. To me, love looks like sacrifice. It looks like change because the person you love today will not be the same person tomorrow. People evolve and unless you evolve with them, the relationship will dissolve. Your mate will need something different daily. Love is consistent and being attentive. Love is the ability to love sacrificially, even when it's uncomfortable.

"While evolution is necessary, so is one's ability to control their thoughts, ideas, and actions."

Stand Up and Protect Your Dreams

"We derive from a culture founded on oppression. But; we have evolved, which is why you must choose success and FREEDOM."

The most powerful thing in this world is a question. Often times, the answers you need are right before you, but; if the question never presents itself then the answer is useless. As my friend and I were walking home from the bus stop one day, I asked her did she think it was possible to really become anything we wanted to be in life. She replied to me "Tamika, always Dream Big, and Believe in Miracles because anything can happen." She was killed in January 2016 and of all the memories we created, that conversation is the one memory that has stayed with me since I was fifteen years old. What I didn't understand at fifteen was that aside from having big dreams, I needed to create a plan and invest in my vision. As I journeyed through life, I learned the importance of creating a plan and capturing my vision on paper. I also learned that there were going to be far more adversaries than supporters along the way. Often times we all struggle to realize what our dreams are, but; I knew what my dreams were at a very young age. It wasn't until I was an adult that I realized what my purpose was and it aligned with my dreams.

I am an unfiltered example of why one should never give up on your dreams because you own them and have the right to execute them.

Although I counted myself out more times than one can imagine, I've always had favor over my life. One of the many reasons that I never gave up was because I inherited five beautiful children from God, who are constantly watching me and look to me for guidance. What I realized a long time ago was that my children couldn't really be who they wanted to be unless I was who God needed me to be. I am the example of the woman that my daughters will someday aspire to become. I am the example of the woman that my sons will someday want to marry. Most importantly, I am the model, the foundation and the blueprint to their success. As a single mom, I knew that it was incumbent upon me to "Stand Up and Protect My Dreams." Otherwise, my children would never witness resilience, hard work, faith, hope, success, a warrior, a Christ Representer, a woman who serves from the rear, leads from the front, and most importantly a woman of courage!

For two consecutive years after I experienced my first bout with lupus anticoagulant, I became extremely sick, battled depression, and lost faith. I felt trapped in a hopeless situation. I would lie in my bed in the most excruciating pain thinking that it would be so much easier to simply give up and die. There were some nights that I would be so consumed by the noise in my head that I thought I was about to lose my mind. When I became quieter with hope of hiding my depression, the noise became louder and louder. With every trial and every tribulation that I experienced, it became harder and harder to silence the noise. During this time, I was battling with more than six medical elements, two of which were life threatening and I began to feel defeated. When depression sets in, you begin to lose your desire to live and if you're not careful, you will be consumed by that which manifest. After more than two years of being in a period of stagnation, I woke up one morning and said to myself, Tamika you have to train your soul to desire what it is that you really want because this isn't the life that God has for you. I realized I had so many unfulfilled dreams and in order for me to accomplish them, I had to stand up and protect my dreams. One of those dreams was to someday become a published author.

In life you must set goals and be sure to write them down so that you have a sense of direction, a point of reference, and a reminder of where you want to go in life. Goals should be living documents and trigger you to work harder than you ever have before. When God placed it on me to write this book on March 1, 2010, I documented it as a goal, used it as a metric, enlisted support by sharing my goals and intention with my family and friends (so that they would hold me accountable) and then I began to execute my goals, one-by-one, because having a goal without putting in the work is simply reliving a fantasy over and over again.

There were times where I desired what I didn't have and took for granted opportunities that were right before me because I confused having things that I wanted with making it to top. I worked for monetary rewards and neglected to see the opportunities that could have taken me to unprecedented levels of success. There should always be a direct connection between your purpose and your success! Although I was happy working in corporate America, I realized that success wasn't given even when I worked extremely hard. I got a paycheck, which was my reward for a job well done. I also learned that the path to success is never straight. It's a winding road with various detours that lead to your destination. I had so many people doubt me, tell me that I would fail at success, and that I would never finish this book. I learned to live in the battle of words because victory isn't trying to change the minds of your adversaries, but; letting them doubt you so that God's word proves to be stronger than their assumptions. I stood firm and praised my way through every test, trial, and tribulation because the intensity of your praise dictates the intensity of your faith. You're going to make mistakes along the way and the moment that you want to forget those mistakes will be the very moment that someone will remember. Continue to hold your head high and when they reminisce, simply smile and say we live and we learn. Just thank God for the lesson taken from that mistake and where you've been because where you've been doesn't determine who you are or where you're headed.

The most important thing to remember when it comes to protecting your dreams is your ability to recognize what an opportunity is. In my opinion, an opportunity doesn't always come in the form of money or recognition for a job well done. It may come in the form of a total stranger that you encounter in a grocery store, who you'll hold a general conversation with that turns into a lifelong friendship. Remember to get out of your own way. Often times we get so caught up on what everyone else is doing, saying and presenting that we lose sight of purpose and don't exercise our passion (which is what drives us to our purpose.) Don't compromise under pressure because you will begin to worry about problems that haven't even presented themselves and worry is a definite sign of disbelief. Don't allow your dreams to be buried by fear, finances or defeat. Make a firm decision to come out of your tomb (spiritual metaphor for a cage.)

Lastly, be BOLD and FIRM! Make sure that you have FUN while protecting your dreams. With all the education, resources, reinforcement and student loans we have the ability to not sit still waiting for someone to give you a job. Implement what you have learned and apply the science of business, success, and survival. We have the natural ability to survive through trial and error. Stop training others to do what you are called to do. Be unconventional and walk BOLDLY in the authority that you have been given! Remember that when you do something unconventional and bold, you must expect both negative feedback and backlash from people. I walk BOLDLY because at the end of this life, I will look back over it and know that I truly LIVED and owned my days.

Regardless of whether they were great, horrible or indifferent, they belonged to me and I walked away with so much to include fulfilled dreams.

"When you're passionate about fulfilling your purpose, you'll walk in it. When it's your destiny, you won't stop until you reach it."

Standing in the Gaps

**"Turmoil and conflict is the absence
of both peace and God."**

In my opinion, standing in the gaps is a spiritual reference made when one intercedes by warring in the spirit on behalf of another. Having an authentic relationship with God is necessary for intercessors as intercessors are essential to life. I've had plenty of people war on my behalf during difficult times. Unfortunately, there comes a time in each of our lives when we will experience a storm. Storms generally derive from chaos as a result of our disobedience to God or us simply ignoring all the signs around us. There are also cases where there's a storm raging, because someone has come into our lives and shook it up. Often times, God will allow you to go through storms to put something in you that you wouldn't have had if you didn't go through that storm. During this time, everything is tested to include your faith, your family, your friendships, your strength, and most importantly your relationship with God will be tested. The storm isn't designed to take you out, but, instead it's designed to lift you up in the very face of those who doubted you and counted you out. Scientifically, the quietist place in a storm is in the eye of it, which is a representation of the center of the storm. If you learn to pray and trust God while you're in the eye of the storm and keep your eyes on God who's the storm chaser, He will keep you during the storm. What I have learned is that when you specialize in taking on other people's problems, you must first make sure you have a firm relationship with God, as He is your personal counselor and place of refuge. Before I learned this, often times I would feel the burden of being what I felt was a "dumping ground" for just about every person I came in contact with in life. When I first began seeing my clinical psychologist she explained that every psychiatrist needs a psychiatrist. Now I understand why.

What I love is that my gift is an inheritance. My matriarchs prayed fervently and "Stood in The Gaps" for a multitude of people. They passed on this unwavering desire to help everyone and to save the world (metaphorically.) I remember the first time I felt the need to "stand in the gaps" for someone and it proved to be the hardest of them all because I was attempting to do something that I had never done before. I had no clue as to what I was doing. I just knew that I worshipped my older sister and life was changing rapidly, day-by-day. The relationship that I had with my sister can be described in one word, AUTHENTIC. I've yet to experience this type of relationship again. We were sisters by birthright and we were best friends by choice. She was a woman who's walk commanded love, respect and she brought joy to every person she encountered. It goes without saying that we had a bond that no one was capable of breaking and we were spiritually inseparable. She was always so focused, responsible and strong. As long as I could remember, I always admired my sister and as I witnessed her fight for her life in 2003, what I admired most was "the fight in her." She fought silently until her death on September 10, 2003.

On September 8, 2003, as I stood next to her she grabbed my hand and asked me to sit on the side of her hospital bed next to her. I did as she asked, well ordered (LOL) and when I did, she refused to let me get up not even to go to the bathroom. What was so profound about this moment was that she didn't want to talk to me, she just wanted me sit in silence as she held my hand. All I can remember is me saying to myself is "Don't Cry Tamika." I still remember how soft and warm her hands felt. As I sit here reflecting and writing this chapter, I had to take a minute to close my eyes, to remember that moment. The tears began to flow because although I will never get an opportunity to experience that feeling again, I wish I understood the value of silence at that very moment. Silence enables one to hear unspoken words. I witnessed my sister and my grandmother sit for more than three hours holding hands without uttering a word. I watched my grandma gaze into my sisters' eyes for hours while sitting at her bedside in her wheelchair. My grandmother has an anointing on her and I always knew that she was a woman of faith who possessed a gift; but, I saw God in her that very day. I have replayed the events leading up to my sister's death a million times and will NEVER understand her battle. I began to pray like I had never prayed before. I called on my cousin to pray with me because for once I feared what was about to happen and I didn't have an understanding of a sincere relationship with God at that time.

The moment I believe that my mom's heart sank was when she walked in the room and my sister said to her, "Ma, I'm ready to fight. Tell me what I need to do to fight." By this time, it was too late, but; my mom said to her, "You need to eat." I can't imagine how my mother felt in that moment because I've never asked her, but; she showed me what hope, strength and love looked like in that very moment. My sister's fight was coming to an end and God was on His way to take back what was His. I heard others "stand in the gap" for her like the women my Aunt Wannie sent up to pray over her. Before they prayed, they asked any non-believers to exit the room. No one moved and they began to pray for her. They started "speaking in tongue" as they prayed over my sister who was incoherent at the time they did, my sister's body raised up off of the bed. Again, she hadn't opened her eyes for nearly twenty-four hours prior. Just before she took her last breath, we watched my sister raise both of her hands as straight as boards to the heavens, and then we watched my sister take her last breath, surrounded by LOVE. Just as she took her last breath, we thought for sure it was done. She started to breathe again. My mom said, "come on Nee-Nee" and I was relieved. Moments later, she took her last breath again and this time it was done. I remember my mom saying, "that's it" and finally I saw the tears begin to flow freely down her cheeks. I immediately placed my right hand on her heart and experienced the most amazing gift. I felt one beat, then another beat, then another beat, and then the last beat of her heart hit the palm of my hand like a beating drum. For three seconds, my heart slowed down to beat in unison with hers and that changed the condition of my heart for a very long time. Love had just been snatched from my heart as I watched the Heavens open up for an Angel. Watching my sister die and feeling those last four beats of her heart was one of the two things that really impacted me spiritually and helped to shape my prayer life. It also taught me that prayer was just a conversation between you and God. Not a scripted monologue.

Every trial I went through taught me how to fight. 2 Corinthians 10:4 says that, "For the weapons of our warfare are not carnal, but mighty through God to the pulling down of strong holds." Physically grabbing a weapon wasn't the answer. My family has been under attack for the last year and I was prepared to "stand in the gaps" for those I love. In July of 2015, my cousin had a brain aneurism and a massive stroke. From the moment I got the news, I began to war on her behalf. While we spent numerous days in the family room of ICU, we met several people. I couldn't go from the fourth floor family room to the cafeteria without running into one of the many friends that I made during our stay there. I began to stand in the gaps for the loved ones of all of the families we met. Most were fighting for their lives. I still maintain contact with a couple of the families to this very day. I love people and it's evident in my walk. Regardless of where I am, God sends me people from all walks of life and I don't take that for granted.

On a warm summer morning in August of 2015, my nephew, who is the son of my sister who passed in 2003, was shot in the face in the middle of Adams Morgan in Washington, DC. When I learned of this incident, I was on the football field waiting for my children's game to start, but; I immediately dropped everything, jumped in my truck, and began to plead the blood of Jesus over his life. I prayed, worshiped and praised God for protection, healing and strength on the ride to the hospital. It was the longest ride ever from Laplata, MD to Washington, DC. By the time I got there, I knew he was going to live and not die. My family rotated nights staying with him at the hospital, and I chose the first night simply because I planned to sit there and pray ALL NIGHT LONG. Looking at him was a delicate reminder that God is REAL and His mercy is incomparable and unexplainable.

The reason that I said my family was being attacked is because while my nephew was beating the odds daily, my sister was on the very same floor fighting for her life after being diagnosed with stage four cancer. They were on the very same floor. I remember having to go down to her room to let her know what was going on and that he was in ICU. Immediately, she said "take me down there." She was in pain, weak and fighting, but; her concern shifted to him. I asked the nurse for a wheelchair and took her to his bedside. He reached out for her hand and she said to him "we're both going to be alright!" The sacrifice of a warrior is to be admired because it takes a strong person to set aside their trials and tests to fight for someone else.

Shortly after my nephew was discharged and my sister kicked cancer's butt, God decided it was time to pick another delicate flower from this garden of life. As an intercessor and a woman that has a gift, sometimes it's difficult because I can feel death approaching and "standing in the gaps" becomes a challenge when they're close to you. As my sister and I were sitting in the hallway of George Washington University Hospital, I grabbed her hand and began praying out loud declaring healing but; in the middle of my prayer God said to me, "I'm about to take him." I looked at my sister and said, "God needs some time with him." I couldn't just look at my sister who had already lost one husband twenty years prior and say God is about to take another husband and the love of your life. Less than three minutes after we said AMEN, we heard "CODE BLUE ICU 4South." Doctors came running from everywhere and I knew what was happening. A nurse came out and told us that they were trying to save his life and asked us if we wanted to come and watch what they were doing. We said yes and followed the nurse to the back. As my sister, her father-in-law, and I watched more than fifteen people work diligently to save his life before our eyes, I was pleading with God to change His mind. I knew that I was out of order for such a request, but; I knew the man he was to my sister, his children, and grandchildren. He was also my sons' godfather and losing him hurt my son.

After we buried my brother-in-law, a few months later I received a call from my mother early one morning saying my oldest brother was being rushed by ambulance to the hospital. She wasn't sure what his status was at that moment. By the time I got to the hospital, I found out that he had a stroke. I looked to the heavens and silently said, "God, thank you for sheer mercy and grace." He was still alive and that's all that mattered to me. My family stands in strength so I was sure that we could get through any challenges he would face together. I smeared God's name all over my declarations and stood in expectancy because faith is belief without evidence.

In my opinion, "standing in the gaps" is when a person stands in strength with someone else. "Standing in the Gaps" doesn't just have to happen during a tragic life event. In June 2014, my oldest son decided that he was ready to make a public profession of his faith and love for Christ by choosing to be baptized. Just a few days before his baptism, I learned that his coach, mentor and honorary uncle, Jason was scheduled to be baptized on the very same day. When I told my son, he was so excited because from the time he met Coach Jason, he took a special liking to him and viewed him as a father figure. At that time Rashard's father had been absent, for two consecutive years so this relationship that extended beyond the football field was very important to him. Dozens of my relatives came out to witness his baptism and then immediately following, Coach Jason took Rashard to dinner. It was just the two of them so that they could talk. While I will probably never know what they talked about, what I do know is that it was of substance. Men like my brothers, adult nephews, and Coach Jason have remained consistent and have continued to "stand in the gaps" in the continued absence of his father.

Writing this chapter was the hardest part of this book, as well as; the most therapeutic because although I lost my first best friend and to capture it in words almost felt impossible. I was able to and I have learned a great deal about life, death and spiritual gifts. I remember what it felt like when I was fighting for my life. I never felt alone and I didn't want them to feel that way either. I knew that I had warriors "standing in the gaps" for me but I had cultivated a powerful prayer life and had a direct connection to divinity.

Hide ME

> **"Hear my voice, oh god, in my complaint;
> preserve my life from dread of the enemy. Hide
> me from this secret council of evildoers."**
> **PSALM 64:1-2**

During the course of my life, I've thought, said and done some things that I'm not proud of, but; the vast majority of those things have been a contributing benefactor to the woman that I have evolved into today. The one thing I have done consistently throughout the course of my life is motivate, inspire and encourage others. In the midst of encouraging, motivating and inspiring people, I found myself taking on their burdens and in some cases; I began to take on their demons, which made my sleeping demons rise. I didn't understand the impact of counseling others without seeking counsel for myself. Subconsciously, I guess I never wanted to seek counsel because like most, I wasn't eager to discuss my dark secrets, fears and failures. I didn't want to feel like I was weak or like I didn't have control over my thoughts and my life. After all, I had it all together, or at least I thought I did. I didn't realize that it was God hiding me. Although I elected not to go through any type of counseling when I was clearly suffering inside, I did encounter a multitude of people who poured into me as much as I was pouring into others. Often times I was surrounded by powerful, ambitious women, who were suffering with things themselves, but; still persevered.

One day while riding to visit my sister in Chantilly, Virginia, I was talking to my niece about a title for this book. I was telling her that I needed a title that really defined who I am. I began to pray silently for God to give me a title for my book. I wanted a title that had substance and was meaningful. Less than two minutes into the prayer, a little voice spoke to my heart and said "Hide Me!" I blurted it out to my niece and she looked at me and said, "I love it!" It was at that moment that I had an idea as to what the title of my book would be. It wasn't until God confirmed it that I understood why. A couple of weeks later, I was sitting on my mother's living room floor writing proposed chapters for the book while the kids were occupied. Messiah and Rashard were climbing all over my mother, Heaven was doing homework, and Chase was listening to my mother's iPod. Chase was famous for making us listen to music. He started with my mother and went from one person to another putting the iPod ear buds in our ears so that we could listen to music. When Chase got to me, he said "Mommy, listen to God" as he put the ear buds in my ear. I heard the words "Hide Me" and I immediately snatched the ear buds out. I yelled JESUS, and my mother asked "what's wrong?" I told Chase to "take the iPod to Grandma" and he did. I told her to restart whatever song that was and listen closely. She did and then she looked at me and said, "wow!" I asked her what song it was and she said it was Psalm 64 by Smokie Norful. I had already shared the title with my mother before I heard this song, so this confirmation was mind blowing. I was once told by a Chaplin at George Washington University Hospital to stop running from my calling and to find the scripture that defines me. I immediately began to read Psalm 64 on my phone and it became evident that after years of searching, I had finally found the scripture that defined who "I AM!"

In my world, I feel like there are two people living inside of me. There's the "good" woman who's the rational thinker, insightful, cautious, intellectual, ambitious, considerate, inspirational, motivational and encouraging woman. Then there's that "evil" girl who is manipulative, spontaneous, daring, a risk taker, bold, promiscuous and destructive when provoked. Nearly my entire adult life, I have made decisions that have led me into a life filled with lessons because I have battled between both "good and evil." I have taken risks, trusted strangers with my life and I've stood up for what I believed in even if it meant losing everything. That good girl has protected the evil girl from ruining her and the evil has sheltered the good from other evildoers.

For instance, I recall the first time I decided to try on-line dating, I was finally excited to have a vehicle where I could filter out those brothers who weren't compatible with me prior to having a full fledge conversation. While I realized that the internet allows you to be who you want to be, eventually your representative has to introduce you. It's impossible to pretend forever. My discernment was always on point, but; fear is what kept me safe over the years. I was very selective and when something just didn't feel right, I didn't ignore that tugging at my heart. I remember when I met a brother on a popular online dating site a few years ago. We had amazing conversations, and when we would hang out, we had so much fun, but; there was always this feeling of reservation in my heart. I couldn't even bring myself to kiss him goodnight. Something just didn't sit right with me. One night we were having a serious conversation and I began to talk to him about his health and he kept changing the subject. I felt like he was hiding something, so I decided not to go any further. He tried hard to move forward, while I paid close attention to that tugging in my heart. The more I ran away the more he tried up until Thanksgiving of 2014. That was the last time I received a message from him through Facebook (which was the only way he could reach me). Then in March 2015, I was scrolling through my timeline and there was a RIP above his picture. I looked at it for about 5 minutes before I reached out to his best friend to offer my condolences. At the end of our two-hour conversation, he told me that he never interfered with his homeboy's affairs, but; he was glad when he found out that I stopped seeing him abruptly. I was curious as to why, so I asked. That's when he shared with me that he knew that he had full blown AIDS. I was shocked, but; it explained his efforts to avoid my inquiries about his health and that uncomfortable feeling that just wouldn't go away.

As the tears rolled down my cheeks, I couldn't help but reflect on a hot summer day in 2014. As my children, mom and I were getting out of the car, the ice cream truck was pulling into my mom's housing community. After a long beautiful day together and as the afternoon was coming to an end, I decided to reward Heaven with a treat from the ice cream truck for being so helpful. On my way to the ice cream truck, my phone rang. I recognized the number right away and although I was expecting to hear an automated appointment reminder, I still answered the phone. Surprisingly, when I answered, there was someone on the other end of the phone:

Me: Hello

Paige: Hello Ms. Benbow, how are you? This is Paige from Dr. Dent's office.

Me: I'm fine, thanks for asking! What can I do for you?

Paige: Dr. Dent needs to see you in her office for a follow up visit for the lab work you had done last Friday.

Me: Ok.

Paige: Are you free to come in on Tuesday at 11 am?

Me: Yes.

Paige: Great, we will see you then.

Me: You have me a little scared.

Paige: Don't be scared, there's no reason to be scared Ms. Benbow, Dr. Dent just needs to talk to you.

Me: Am I ok? Because I've never gotten a call like this from her office. Do I have AIDS or HIV?

Paige: Did you have that test performed?

Me: Yes, I requested an HIV test and signed the form to be tested.

Paige: Hold on one second.

As I held the phone waiting in anticipation for her response, I immediately began to reflect on the careless choices I made and my reckless behavior. I could hear Paige flipping through pages and what was only about a minute felt like an eternity.

Paige: Ms. Benbow.
Me: Yes.
Paige: Yes, you do.
Me: Oh my God…I'm HIV positive?
Paige: Yes, you are; I'm so sorry Ms. Benbow.
Me: No…I can't believe this, oh my God, oh my God.

I was hot from head to toe. I forgot about the ice cream truck and the fact that Heaven was standing directly behind me. My world collapsed at that very moment. All I could think of was the man that I trusted with my life and that Karma had finally grabbed hold of me with both hands. Where do I go from here? I was filled with a flood of emotions. I remembered thinking that the scariest part of this is that when you contract a disease such as HIV and Herpes even, you're immediately reduced to the condition of your circumstances.

Paige: I'm just kidding.
Me: I'm going to kill you, my heart just dropped.
Paige: You have to be more careful, if you're that scared.

She was right. I had to be more careful. I know a lot of people who are dealing with these elements so it's real to me and a delicate subject for many. Listening to that little voice that kept saying, "something just isn't right," kept me safe, but; it didn't stop me from taking risks. As a matter of fact, shortly after this scare, I met a man at my aunt's retirement party. He was tall, dark and handsome. He captured my attention before he approached me. I think he strategically made certain we had a moment alone, just long enough to get my number. Shortly after meeting him, we had sex and needless to say, that reckless "little girl" inside of me was uninhibited and naïve. I trusted another man with my life with no defined commitment, which is always dangerous. I just knew that he was seeing someone else simply because I was. I was using protection with the other gentleman because he was what I considered a filler, which was the person who filled in for the one I actually wanted when I couldn't have him. When my thoughts began to wander, so did I. Because I suffered from multiple medical elements, two of which are life threatening, I had to see my hematologist weekly during that time. So during a routine Thursday afternoon visit, I asked for another HIV test which became a harmless joke between me and a couple of the lab technicians. Subconsciously, I wasn't concerned, but; I trusted someone with my life and I only knew what he shared with me. The next day I went to work as usual, and when I was in work mode, my personal phone stayed in my purse in the closet and my government cell stayed on my hip or in my hand. When I finally left for the day, I checked my phone and realized that I had missed a call from my doctor's office. There was a voice mail from a nurse asking me to call the office when I got the message. I looked at the clock and when I saw 6:45 pm, I immediately started to have a panic attack. That feeling was an indicator and reminder that I was living recklessly again.

Throughout the course of the night, I started to notice all of the symptoms associated with HIV/AIDS. The next morning, I called one of the lab technicians and she didn't know anything. My anxiety grew even stronger and I lashed out at him. The one I didn't trust and who shouldn't have trusted me caught the blunt of my anger. I knew I had to pull it together because my sister-friend was celebrating her upcoming nuptials and I had to be in full support, smiles and all. Of course, I called Becky (my accountability partner) who assured me that she would go with me on Monday morning to make sure I was okay. Oddly, I had an amazing time with six amazing women who made me forget about my anxiety for a few hours. As soon as I left, I called the bride to be and thanked her for a great night and told her what I was going through. She prayed for me and we talked for a while. She's always had a way of calming me down. Outside of my grandmothers and older women in my family, she was the first real "Woman of God" (WOG) who I looked to for the truth, especially when it was uncomfortable. After we hung up, I got a good night's rest and then Sunday was a day filled with worship and tears or repentance or regret I should say. I found myself begging God to forgive me and to perform another miracle. I was praying for an answer that only He had.

Monday morning couldn't come soon enough and I made sure I was there when they opened at 7am. Becky and I met up there, but; because I was anxious, I went straight to a nurse and told her I missed a call on Friday and that a nurse that I wasn't familiar with left me a voicemail. The nurse went to the back to talk to my doctors to see if he had a minute for an impromptu visit. He did and I was relieved. When he walked in the room, he didn't waste any time. He said, "You're fine, I told her to call you and tell you that everything was okay because I know how you are." There was a sigh of relief and an intimate moment between God and I.

I've said, thought and felt things that others would be too ashamed to reflect upon, let alone even document. I shared because as my pastor says, "your scars are the answer to someone else's question." God has hidden me from a great deal as I have journeyed through life risking it all.

"Let my life be your lesson."

Three Days

"I believe that whatever you subconsciously believe to be real in your dreams; IS."

Theoretically, some would compare a near death experience or a transition onto the other side to "hallucination." I believe that a near death experience is comparable to an unstoppable force meeting an immovable object that's filled indescribable moments. I also believe that transitioning over onto the other side is unprecedented and an experience that God is certainly at the center of. While most fear the unknown and wouldn't care to hear how real God is, there are others who are interested because it's the closest they'll ever come to experiencing the power of God. In this chapter, I will explore the events of various seasons over the course of a five-year period leading up to the day that changed my life. Although I've experienced so much in life, nothing would compare to the season when I discovered that there's life beyond this one.

In 2007, when I decided to start going to church consistently I developed a hunger for knowledge and wanted a clearer understanding of Christianity. I knew that my children needed to attend church regularly since I had only taught them to pray. I hadn't taught them much about God, Jesus and the Holy Spirit, simply because I didn't have an understanding of the Holy Trinity myself. At this time, I only had three children ranging from two to five years of age. I learned that "if it doesn't grab you, don't grab it," so I ended up church hopping for a year before I discovered my current church. When I decided to join I got my babies up and dressed for church just about every Sunday. On those Sunday mornings that I didn't feel like going, my children's desire to go, motivated me to get up and head into the house of The Lord anyway. The moment I would walk through the doors, I would almost immediately become overjoyed that I decided to go. I began to cultivate a practice of worshipping God regularly and I developed a strong spiritual relationship. I was still navigating through life and although my journey was NEW, it wasn't without sin.

In 2009, I was still straddling the fence. I had one foot in the world and one foot in the word. I was working Monday through Friday, partying on Friday and Saturday night and then worshipping on Sunday. I had gotten to a point where I knew who God was, and I believed in Him, but; I had never experienced the Holy Spirit. In 2009, I became pregnant with my 5th child and I was devastated. He wasn't planned and I used contraceptives so I was shocked when I found out I was pregnant. He was the fifth and I decided that he would be the last of my children until I was remarried. While he was unplanned, he was certainly a gift, a blessing and a vessel used to save my life.

On February 15, 2010, my labor was induced. After several hours of labor, we discovered that the baby was grabbing the umbilical cord. Every time I had a strong contraction the baby grabbed the cord which was preventing the flow of oxygen to his brain. After watching him do it in the ultrasound a couple of times, my doctor thought it was safer to deliver him by performing a cesarean (C-section). I didn't want to trifle around with his life, so I agreed to have my first C-section and we immediately headed into the operating room. After giving birth to Chase Alexander, we discovered that he was almost 12lbs and 22 ½ inches long, which may have contributed to my inability to deliver him naturally. I recall having a pleasant stay in the hospital until the day I was discharged. I was running a fever the day before, but; on the day I was discharged, I recall having this breathtaking pain shoot through my abdomen a few times. I told my nurse, and she said perhaps it was just new pain because it was my first C-section. So I was discharged not knowing that "my journey to the other side" had begun. When I was discharged, I went home with my baby boy and my sister kept my other children at my mother's house to give me a few days with him. I was used to going back to work two weeks after every child, but; this time was a little different because this was definitely new pain. I immediately started the process to live a healthier life by eating salads, fruit and drinking nothing but cranberry juice and water. I was breastfeeding so this was very important to me. I wanted a healthy baby as well and unfortunately, he was my fourth baby to come home severely jaundice.

Day One

On February 23, 2010, I took Chase to get his bilirubin levels (which is used to indicate different types of liver problems) checked and decided to take him to my mother-in-law's house so that she could anoint and pray over him, as she did the three children before him. My sister-in-law, Kris and I would joke about her doing the whole "lion king" thing to my children. This time was so important because I was afraid. I felt death approaching and I just knew that God was about to take my baby. I expressed my concerns to Mother Green before she began to pray. She took Chase out of my arms and lifted him in the air and began to pray fervently. As she prayed, I cried and cried because the spirit of death was so heavy on my heart. When Chase was born, he came out with a frown on his face and it never changed until I saw him smile at the very end of Mother Green's prayer. She looked at me and said, "He's the one." I thought to myself, I hope so because I felt death knocking. We talked for a little bit and then I headed home. When I got in the house and got settled, that uncomfortable feeling consumed me. So much so, that I got on my knees and began to pray harder than I had ever prayed before. I remembered being on my knees asking God for a personal encounter with Him and while I was on my knees, I said "God, I've been on my knees before for all the wrong people and reasons, but; this time is different. I need you to work a miracle." I needed Him to save my baby. I wanted to have a personal encounter with Him. I wanted to see the face of God because I needed to know that He was real. In the middle of praying I must've fallen asleep because I woke up on my knees (bedside) to Chase crying. I jumped up and looked at the clock and realized it was feeding time. He was a huge baby and needed to eat every two hours around the clock, especially since I needed him to make as many bowel movements as possible to cleanse his little system. As soon as I was done feeding him, I burped him, changed him, prayed over him and laid him down next to me. It was time for me to catch a nap before his next feeding, but; Chase wasn't having it.

Every time I would lie down, Chase would scream to the top of his lungs. I grew concerned because he hadn't cried like that in the nine days that he had been on earth. I knew he wasn't hungry, wet or gassy. I mean, I had only done this four time before him. I sat up anyway, picked him up and rocked him until he was comfortable and sleep again. I laid him down again and as soon as I would lie down beside him, he would begin to scream again. This happened multiple times and by the time I made my fifth attempt to lay him down, it was 4:30 am. By this time, I was really concerned, but; I knew that I had a 7:30 am appointment with my OBGYN, to have my staples removed. I decided to wrap his "boppy" around my waist and just hold him while he slept. I sat upright with intentions to get some rest, but; I coughed the entire night and throughout the morning, I didn't manage to get much rest. I had gone nearly twenty-four hours with very little rest.

Day Two

When I woke up, I was short of breath and coughing like I needed to bring something up, but, couldn't. I was also having strong heart palpitations that became very uncomfortable. I went to my doctor's appointment as planned, and told her about the symptoms I was having. She listened to my heart and heard what's called PVC's (premature ventricular contractions.) She immediately tried to find a cardiologist willing to see me as soon as possible. After spending four hours in her office while she worked diligently to find someone to see me, she said to me "Baby, you know your body and if something doesn't feel right, go to the emergency room, right next door." I still had to take the baby to get his levels checked again, so I told her I would do it as soon as I took him to his appointment. Leaving her office, I realized that walking from her office to my car, which was less than twenty feet, was exhausting and I couldn't breathe. I was gasping for air, but; I was determined to take my baby to his appointment, at Southern Maryland Hospital to get his blood drawn. As soon as we were done, I went to my mother's house to see my children, who I hadn't seen since I was in the hospital. They were so excited to see me and although I didn't feel well, I put a happy face on and loved on my babies. At one point, my sister who was keeping them started yelling and cursing at them and it really hit a nerve because I was paying her to take care of them and she was being mean. I said to her "they miss me and that's why they're hype." I got so agitated that I stood up and said "I'm going to take them home so that you don't have to deal with them anymore." That was frustration talking because I paid her $500 to keep them and I was annoyed that she was that impatient. While I was standing there, I got real dizzy and there was a tugging at my heart. A tiny voice said, "Don't do it, go to the emergency room now." At that very moment, my niece (who's like my daughter) walked in from school. I asked her to take care of Chase while I went to the ER to get checked out and hopefully get some antibiotics (because you know we think antibiotics take care of everything.) She said yes, and jumped in the shower while I warmed up his bottle and changed him. When I left my children, my plan was to be seen, get a prescription and to take them home with me that night.

When I signed in at the hospital, there was no wait so they triaged me right away. The nurse looked at me and said, "are you in any pain," and I replied by saying "no ma'am." As tears began to roll down my cheeks, she stood up and said, "Come with me." We walked to the back when a nurse and two doctors came in immediately and began to ask me questions. One of the doctors looked at me and said, "Your heart is only beating at 38 bpm and the average heart beats at 70 bpm." All I knew was that I was having trouble breathing. The doctor had them run an electrocardiogram (EKG) on me and ordered a CT Scan with contrast. I was medically well versed so I understood what she was asking for, but; I didn't know why. A technician came within minutes to take me to radiology. I had the CT Scan and the radiologist talked to me the entire time. I believe he could tell that I was nervous. I asked him if I was okay, and he grabbed my hand and said, "You're going to be fine." That put me at ease until the two doctors came back into my room and told me that my results were back. One of the doctors asked me if I came alone and I explained to her that I did in fact drive myself. They then asked where my children were and if there was someone that they could call because they couldn't guarantee that I would make it through the night. They explained to me that I had massive bilateral pulmonary embolisms (which was the medical term for abnormally large blood clots in both lungs) and a weak heart. By this time, my heart rate slowed down more and my blood pressure was really low. I will never forget one doctor saying to me "I don't know how you're walking around; your body is half dead."

The doctors stepped out and as I began to cry, the nurse said to me "don't cry, that'll make it worse, just pray." At that moment, I couldn't find the words to pray. The only thing I could think about were my children because I didn't like the way my sister was treating them. I asked her for a phone because my cell phone was dead. She came back with the phone and I made a few calls. One call was to my mother, and the others were to my ex-husband and the father of my son. My mother got to the hospital in less than twenty minutes and my ex-husband and my son's dad picked their children up from my mother's house. By the time my mother got there, the doctors had already given me a choice of hospitals because they didn't feel comfortable caring for me, since there was nothing they could do to save my life. They gave me a choice of going to a community hospital in Laplata, MD or a "school of medicine" in DC. Although I liked the "school of medicine," I elected to go to the community hospital because it's a "traveling hospital," which means that physicians from all over the world practice there and many specialize in something (the heart and blood in my case.) I told my mother that she could go take care of my ten-day old baby because there was nothing that she could do for me there. My mother refused to leave me until the ambulance got there to transport me. After the ambulance arrived, my mother left and I was transported to the "community hospital."

When I arrived, they put me in room where I had to be monitored around the clock. There were at least four people watching monitors and in and out of my room every ten to fifteen minutes. Shortly before 9:30 pm a nurse practitioner (NP) came in and answered all of my questions. The very first question I asked her was "Am I going to live?" She replied by saying, "I will tell you that we're going to do everything in our power to make you comfortable and our goal is to keep you alive, but; embolisms can sometimes, take on a course of their own." She also said, "Because your clots are so large, you can't get out of the bed not even to use the bathroom." The NP went on to say, "We'd prefer it if you moved as little as possible because we don't want to do anything that will cause them to shift." After speaking with her, my nurse Lindsey came in and she promised me that she wasn't going home until

I felt comfortable. She came in throughout the night just to check in on me.

Day Three

Throughout the night, they gave me morphine (for comfort), Xanax (for anxiety) and dilaudid (for pain) and none of it helped me to rest. I was on day three with no sleep. I was extremely tired, but; I was determined to get every prayer out of me. If I was going to die, God was going to hear every concern, secret thought and request I had in me. I was determined to hold on until my prayers were answered or until He was ready for me. At approximately 3:30 am, something happened and I can only give you an account of it, because it was so powerful that it's difficult to explain. I began to feel really warm all over and at first I felt like I was beginning to drift into a deep sleep, but; then I felt like I was suffocating. I could feel myself slipping away. As I reached for the call button, an unstoppable force pulled my hand back, I tried to call Lindsey's name, but; nothing would come out. Then it happened, I saw a bright light beaming and as I began to reach, I heard a calm, but; firm voice (that still brings tears to my eyes) say "not yet my child." In the midst of all of the chaos that I could hear all around me, this voice was so clear and comforting. I could also hear Lindsey say, "No, I promised her that she'd go home to her five children." At that moment, I managed to open my eyes. There were at least ten to fifteen people in my room scattering. One doctor at the foot of my bed was calling my name and one was on my bed holding a syringe filled with atropine (which is a drug used to increase the *heart* rate and improve the atrioventricular conduction by blocking the parasympathetic influences on the *heart*.) This was kept in my room on the sink. When I came to, I asked them what they were doing and the doctor at the foot of my bed said, "We lost you there for a minute." I looked at him and said, "I was just resting." He replied saying, "you were resting alright, now how many fingers am I holding up?" I said "five" and he said "no, four because this is a thumb'" and a handful of them laughed. I looked at Lindsey and she came right over with a hand full of tissue and began to wipe my face. Tears were flowing down my cheeks and I didn't even feel it. She said, "You scared me!" I apologized and said, "That scared me too!" Later that morning, my sister and brother-in-law (who died in 2015) were my first visitors and by this time I was just excited to be alive yet too tired to engage. It was on the third day that I was chosen to live and not die.

Death is certainly a part of life and the only thing that's guaranteed. We will all die someday and unfortunately, it's not something that you can prepare for. Having lost so many people throughout my life, I used to fear death. It wasn't until I nearly died that I was set free from my fear of dying. Death causes you to STOP. It forces you to reflect on your life, the direction of your future and causes you to evaluate past, current and future relationships. While I was in transition onto the other side, I had a million thoughts, especially since I could hear everything that was going on around me. It's been said that your hearing is the last thing to go when you're transitioning. I can confirm this to be true. I've experienced things that some will never understand and that I will never forget. I recall having a conversation with the Chaplin during my stay and she said "I believe that God deals with us on our time and our terms." It was at that moment that it all made sense. Personally, I believe that Jesus does meet us where we are. Just think for a moment, in the various stories in the books of the Bible, Jesus was found in the valleys and the low places with those who others saw as the unusable.

After this encounter for the very first time in my life, I trusted God. During this time, I was on fire for him, I loved him and I had so much faith in HIS ability. My faith did not waiver and I believed everything that GOD said he would do for me. My GOD delivered on all of his promises of provision, protection and prosperity.

I AM!

"You have to be the balance of power between, who you are and who you really want to be."

I AM a used to be!

I've journeyed through life living as if I were two different people. I'm a woman who tried God and when I felt like He wasn't working, I ran back to Satan because I knew He would take me back. I have done both good and evil, but; never at the same time. Thank God that the things I used to do and the woman I <u>used to be</u> didn't hinder me from becoming the woman I AM today. What I have learned is that the moment that you want to forget who you <u>used to be</u>, will be the very moment that everyone will choose to remember. When I find myself in that position, I just thank God that what I've done, who I've done, and where I've been doesn't determine who I AM or where I'm headed.

I AM intentional in everything I do!

A life without regret isn't a life at all. Everything I do is with intention regardless of what it is. If I'm cooking, it's <u>with the intent</u> of presenting a tasteful dish to my family. If I'm writing, often times it's <u>with the intent</u> of inspiring or encouraging someone. If I'm worshipping, it is <u>with the intent</u> of getting into the presence of God! If I'm playing with my children, <u>it is my intent</u> to create memories! If I'm having a conversation, it is <u>with the intent</u> of learning. That last intent is important to me because I have learned that you should enter into every conversation and situation as a learner. My life is filled with purpose so when I decide to do something, I take it serious because my intention is predicated on my purpose. I believe that whatever your intention is will be where your focus lies. When you're intentional, success comes.

"I AM unapologetically REAL!"

I believe that every influential person is controversial and that controversy creates dialogue. It's like real art...it comes with a hefty price and a great conversation.

"I AM BOLD!"

When you're bold, you LIVE and when you LIVE, you take risks that will take you places you never thought you'd go. I've been everywhere.

I AM Ready For Love!

[Max Lucado once wrote *"A woman's heart should be so hidden in God that a man has to seek Him to find her."*] Any relationship where you plan to see residual on your investment will require a tremendous amount of energy, dedication and an emotional investment. I've experienced love and I definitely know what it looks like. However, I've never been in love with a man. I was once told that because I have such a colorful mind and because I've experienced so much, finding love is going to be a challenge. I agree, but; I'm certainly ready to trust God and the man that He has kept for me. I believe that our inability to be open minded will prevent us from acquiring what we are entitled to.

Love isn't limited to romantic relationships. I've loved without reservation my entire life! Now that I've been stripped down to my truth, I'm ready to be loved!

"I AM a woman who God wanted to use in an extraordinary way...

I'm comfortable with talking about God and witnessing to people the way I do because I've been taught how to. God has dispatched me into the world to be a witness because the tests, trials and longsuffering that I've endured prepared me to stand firm before His people. When you are different and expectations have been laid out for your life, there's a great responsibility to go out into the world and bring back souls to God. I would ask myself, why did He choose me especially after all that I have done? I came to the realization that often times; God will use the weak to lead the strong.

I learned that God doesn't need man to verify the word in my life, so I stopped focusing on my situation because I'll never have it all together. God will purposely choose the one who everyone overlooks so that no man gets credit for His work. God will take a woman with five children (some born out of wedlock), a former whoremonger and a sinner to use her in a way that blows one's mind.

I AM an Ambitious Leader!

A person who doesn't have an original idea is generally incompetent of leading because someone else will always be the influence or motivational force behind their operation. Fortunately, I'm a creative, innovative, visionary, who is an executor. These are good qualities to have in a leader. When you occupy yourself thinking about what you can't do, you miss the opportunity to fully explore what you can do!

I AM Gifted!

I'm comfortable with being ostracized because I'm okay with being set apart from others. When there is something unique about you, I believe that it means that GOD decided to lay grace (your gift and that "thing" that you don't deserve) on you. He has made you different from others for a divine purpose.

I AM Secure (In My Skin) and Guarded!

The most dangerous thing to both men and women is a PLUS SIZED woman who has great confidence in her abilities. A woman who wears confidence will stand out and never fit in.

I AM a Former Whore Monger!

I've dated a wide array of men and often times I've gone for the wrong guy. I made a conscious decision to sleep around on my quest to find what I was missing simply because I wanted to. What I've learned over the years is that you must first become the woman who will attract the man you deserve. Otherwise, you will get the man that you desire and desires are temporary, so in essence, you will be too. Desires only provide temporary fulfillment so there will always be that presence of emptiness. I believe that some men desire vulnerable women because they're open to the unexpected. As a woman, I refused to be vulnerable because I needed to protect my heart. This created a problem because I became desensitized to men and I became a whoremonger in the process because when sex became easy to get, love became harder to find. I would sleep with a man and if he didn't satisfy my desires, I'd call someone to finish what he started. What I didn't understand was that no man would ever satisfy me. I believe that my choice in men stems from my biological father's absence, especially during my adolescent years. My psychological hunger for love from my dad was the reason that I looked for him in every man I chose.

I AM a survivor of domestic violence!

"I have been stripped of everything and I'm still standing"

In the summer of 1997, I met a gentleman who came to my sister's house with his god-sister to pick up her daughter. I was 17 years old at the time and had just graduated from the Laurel Senior High School. He expressed interest in me, but I had a boyfriend (my high school sweetheart.) My friend told me that he was a good guy and that he would take care of me, but since I had a boyfriend I wasn't interested. In 1998, my boyfriend and I broke up and decided that we would be best friends forever. Since I was now a single young woman I decided to date and he was one of the first men that came to mind. Although I dated a few brothers, I have to admit that his god-sister was right when she said that he'd take care of me. He gave me a car to drive, money daily, and sex a few times a day. This was my ideal man. I didn't know he came with a price. I married him (shortly after my 20th birthday) less than 72-hours after he beat me. This was the tenth time that year. I remember that beating on the floor of my bedroom like it was yesterday. After he would beat me, I would listen to music to restore what had been taken. The beat from the instruments would give me strength and the hook would catch me from falling into depression or victim mode just in time to wipe my tears and pick myself back up. Mary J. Blige got me through some of the toughest nights. There were days that I didn't know why he beat me. The one question that I asked myself was "Why?" Why did I allow a man to do the very thing that I despised? Why did I allow a man to rob me of five pregnancies, a joyful pregnancy (with my first born child) and my right to live without fear? These are questions that I don't think I will ever be able to answer. I've heard the opinions of many as to why I stayed, but; I don't think they hold much weight because until you've been in the same position, you don't know why or what you would've done. Every situation is different and no woman is the same. What I do know is that after more than five years of domestic abuse, I had no respect for him. When you lack respect for a man, you become courageous because you no longer care about his feelings.

When I gave birth to our daughter, I knew that I had to leave to protect her. The night I decided that I wasn't going to be a victim anymore was the night that he wrote my name on some bullets and my brother had to intervene. I got a protective order and I packed up my daughter and step-daughters and we moved. Although, I allowed him to stay with me for financial purposes, it took less than 90 days for me to get rid of him. When I left him for good, he wept in front of me. This was something that he had never done before. I didn't even see him cry that hard when his mother died. My mother told me not to fall for the tears and I didn't. I escaped and he went on to abuse his next victim. I forgave him over time and moved on with my life. I never allowed another man to put his hands on me after that last beating and if I saw signs of domestic violence (in any form) I severed ties immediately. What I learned overall is that conflict is never a good thing. Whenever there's conflict, a difference of opinion, and neither party is willing to compromise you should evaluate the situation. When conflict presents itself, find a way to grab your viewpoint with both hands. Place it in your pocket and walk away. You'll find that you walked away with your peace of mind.

I AM a woman who conquered DEPRESSION!

I've lived my life at a euphoric high so when I hit a low point, I didn't quite know how to deal with being in such a low place. I believe that when you lose your desire to live, you begin to die. This has been the toughest season of my life and I've shared my story for the last few years hoping to inspire and encourage someone. For the sake of my sanity, I try my best not to look how I feel. We all have private problems and secret thoughts that we would much rather keep that way. Some of us have that one thing that we don't want anyone to know, and will take to our graves. Unfortunately, we can't plan life. So we all live with something that we'd elect to hide from God, if we could. I've been fighting for a long time and through it all I've managed to help others, but, I've hurt myself in the process. I've always been transparent and will continue to be because that's who I am. Every area of my life was attacked especially my health, independence and finances. I got to a point in my life where I was tired of smiling through pain.

My sister and I had a heart-to-heart one day about people looking at me and assuming that I'm okay. I said to her that I create my happiness because being a mom is the one thing I couldn't prepare for and the one thing I REFUSE TO FAIL AT. My children are my world and because of that, it got to a point where I worried more about them than I did my failing health. The reality of my situation was that I needed help and while people looked at me and thought that I was okay, I really wasn't. I fight daily to stay alive. I was fighting with men to take care of their children, and I felt like I was drowning. I ended up being on anxiety medication and a couple of psychotropic. One of the most uncomfortable things was not being able to control my thoughts and mood.

I woke up one morning and made a conscious decision, NO MORE! I began to pray and took back my life.

I AM a Warrior!

I'm a woman who understands that I bare the scars of my mother, her mother, and her mother's mother. I wear their burdens, their strength, their anger, their intellect, their fight, their courage and their love. Although I have strength, I never really understood how to use it. For a very long time, I tried resolving my problems on my own and found myself giving myself credit when I accomplished what I set out to conquer. As I evolved in my spiritual journey, I realized that praying, praising and worshiping GOD became my spiritual weapons of warfare and God would get all the glory. I began to pray like I had never prayed before. Through prayer I learned that He always heard my prayers, even those quick ten second prayers, when I didn't really want a response. However, it was when I cried out and wept that he gave me direction and understanding. Although I knew that God was ALWAYS listening and answering, at times I refused to listen because he wasn't saying what I wanted to hear.

You can't fight what you can't see! Learning how to war in the spirit is necessary. When you use worldly tactics to wage war you'll lose the battle every time. I learned to war in the spirit and that's when I truly learned to fight.

I AM CHOSEN!

I believe that we all have a purpose in life. As we journey through life leaving footprints, we should do so seeking and ultimately walking in that purpose. The solidarity of walking in your purpose is based on discovering what your purpose is. I believe that your "purpose" is your personalized gift from God. It's the one thing that brings you joy at the thought of it. It's the one thing that you would do for free and not think of being paid for it, because the reward is greater than anything money can buy. It fulfills you and it is used to bless the lives of others. Often times, it can take an eternity for one to actually figure out who they really are, where they're headed, and what their purpose in life is. Many will depart this life without reaching their destiny because they never discovered what their purpose was or was afraid to walk in it. In my lifetime, I've given up a great deal, but; the one thing I refuse to give up is my destiny. After about twenty years of navigating through life, I finally figured out who "I AM." I'm a God fearing, loyal, ambitious, loving and generous woman with flaws who was chosen by God to motivate, encourage and inspire people. While many view flaws as signs of failure, I see flaws as a simple reminder that perfection does not exist here on earth. I also believe that failure is an opportunity to start over. When you know who you are, you don't feel threatened by those who stand next to you. While I've been called many things, I know who I AM.

I love walking in my purpose and sharing knowledge because the only way to reinforce knowledge is to teach someone else.

Citations:

https://www.bible.com/search/bible?q=1%20Peter%20
3:3-4&version_id=1

https://www.bible.com/search/bible?q=Psalm%2064:1-2&version_id=1

51175216R00077

Made in the USA
Middletown, DE
08 November 2017